TURBO-CHARGING
THE HR FUNCTION

Paul Mooney started his working life as a butcher, moved into production management and then held a number of increasingly responsible HR positions at General Electric. He was employed by Sterling Drug as personnel manager during the start-up of their highly successful Irish plant in Waterford before being appointed to the role of human resource director for the Pacific Rim. He holds a PhD (Trinity College) in sociology and undergraduate degrees in industrial relations, and is the author of four other books.

In 1991 he set up PMA Consulting, which specialises in customised organisation and management development programmes. He has now carried out assignments in over 20 countries across five continents; his clients include Hewlett-Packard, Lucent Technologies, the Bank of Ireland, Pepsi, SmithKline Beecham, Statoil and the World Bank.

Other titles in the series:

The Chartered Institute of Personnel and Development is the leading publisher of books and reports for personnel and training professionals, students, and for all those concerned with the effective management and development of people at work. For details of all our titles, please contact the Publishing Department:
tel. 020-8263 3387
fax 020-8263 3850
e-mail publish@cipd.co.uk
The catalogue of all CIPD titles can be viewed on the CIPD website:
www.cipd.co.uk/publications

TURBO-CHARGING THE HR FUNCTION

Paul Mooney

CHARTERED INSTITUTE OF PERSONNEL AND DEVELOPMENT

First published 2001

Design by Paperweight
Typeset by Action Publishing Technology Ltd, Gloucester
Printed in Great Britain by
the Cromwell Press, Trowbridge

British Library Cataloguing in Publication Data
A catalogue record for this book is available from the
British Library

ISBN 0-85292-896-3

Chartered Institute of Personnel and Development,
CIPD House,
Camp Road, London SW19 4UX
Tel: 020 8971 9000   Fax: 020 8263 3333
E-mail: cipd@cipd.co.uk
Website: www.cipd.co.uk
Incorporated by Royal Charter. Registered charity no. 1079797

CONTENTS

DEDICATION

To Amie, Cillian and Nicole – my in-house 'HR team' who
make all the effort worth while.

ACKNOWLEDGEMENTS

I have borrowed ideas from so many different sources that it is difficult to acknowledge individual contributions. Much of this book reflects debates held with client companies and other consultants over the years. Sometimes you win the argument; sometimes you lose. You always walk away with a sharper understanding. Many thanks to the HR directors and line managers who allowed me to 'practise' on their organisations. If I seemed to have had it all figured out in advance – terrific. Most of the time it was the science of muddling through!

I am particularly grateful to those named companies who allowed me to use specific examples in this book from our direct consulting work, because this really helps to illustrate the points made. For reasons of confidentiality others did not wish to be named but hopefully will still see their contribution reflected in the text.

INTRODUCTION

The twentieth century was the age of the machine;
the twenty-first century will be the age of people.
Rosabeth Moss Kanter

What is the rationale for this book?

Almost every recent study of organisational success has high-lighted the critical importance of developing a competent and committed workforce. Yet while most organisations would concur with the statement that 'people are our most important asset', few devote sufficient time and attention to translating this slogan into a working reality.

In practice, effective human resource management is pivotal to successful organisational performance and transformation. However, despite the overwhelming evidence of a positive link between excellence in people management and business success, the HR function has historically been neglected in many organisations. This book sets out to explore why this is so, and to redress the imbalance. It provides a road-map to help organisations develop a powerful 'turbo-charged' HR function which adds real business and organisational value.

What's my line?

One of the underlying issues in the 'strategic neglect' argument is the difficulty of defining the concept of human resource management. Kyle Greer, a Scotsman living for many years in the USA, was my former boss in Sterling Winthrop and a tremendous 'on-the-ground' human resource manager. He related the following story. When his two sons were young boys, they often asked: 'What do you do, Dad?' He tried various explanations about getting line managers to manage their people really well, developing an organisation which would deliver superior performance, etc. It was all to no avail; Kyle's sons remained mystified about his actual job. Eventually he cracked it when he told them that his job was to 'set the price for the food in the canteen'.

Many of us who have spent a lifetime in human resource management are faced with a similar communications challenge. What is our core role? How do we really add value? How can we articulate and measure our contribution to organisations and the people who populate them? Understanding these issues is the route to success in human resource management. The corollary is also true. The absence of an answer to these core questions leaves a vacuum filled by myth and often defamatory comment about the role that HR professionals play in organisations.

Many years ago, Aidan Hope, then financial controller of the General Electric's plant where I worked, nicknamed the personnel function 'the health and happiness department'. When the official title changed to 'human resources', Tom Mangan, another GE veteran, suggested that HR stood for 'human remains' (a name coined during a period of downsizing). While such comment may simply be good-natured banter, it can also mask a real antagonism towards the function – based on the view that there is little value added. There is good cause to believe that this negative view of the HR function is fairly widespread:

> Nestling warm and sleepy in your company, like the asp in Cleopatra's bosom, is a department whose employees spend 80 per cent of their time on routine administration tasks. Nearly every function of this department can be performed more expertly for less by others. Chances are its leaders are unable to describe their contribution to value added except in trendy, unquantified and wannabe terms. Yet, like a serpent unaffected by its own venom, the department frequently dispenses to others advice on how to eliminate work that does not add value ... I am describing, of course, your Human Resources department, and have a modest proposal. Why not blow the sucker up?
>
> Thomas A. Stewart, *Fortune* magazine, January 1996

The profile of the HR function is changing

Whereas the historical picture of the 'added-value' impact of human resources was often negative, in recent years there have been significant changes in the way HR professionals are perceived. There are several reasons that underpin this change.

First, publication of a host of organisational change stories with excellent people management practices at the fulcrum has highlighted the importance of 'human resources' in the 'success mix'.[1] This is reflected in the changing seniority of HR professionals within organisations. A presence in the senior team is now the norm, rather than the exception (the HR director reporting directly to the chief executive rather than through finance or operations). There is also evidence of increasing penetration at board level.[2]

Secondly, in the past three years, salary increases within HR have significantly outstripped those in production, marketing, engineering and finance – highlighting the fact that companies will now pay a premium for talent in this critical area.[3] The changing profile of individuals joining (coupled with retraining of existing HR managers) has deepened the academic pool within the profession[4] and partly explains this rise in salary levels.

Finally, the Institute of Personnel and Development sought and recently acquired 'Chartered Institute' status. The former IPD's own literature draws out the significance of this:

> Becoming a Chartered Institute is the highest accolade any profession can have ... the same status as other premier league professional bodies. In many ways it represents recognition at the highest levels, and a coming of age for our profession.[5]

Given all of the above, it seems utterly clear that this is a crucial moment in the evolution of the human resource function. It is of no surprise, therefore, that the big consulting groups (McKinsey, Andersen Consulting, Boston Consulting Group, etc) are all significantly upgrading their HR practices.[6]

A road-map for superior performance organisations

While such good progress can be acknowledged, tremendous opportunities still exist to reshape the HR function and *modus operandi* within many organisations. This book has been written to address this. It is essentially a practitioner's guide – shaped in the forge of direct human resource management and consulting experience across 20 countries and five continents. It details a step-by-step guide to establishing or reinvigorating an existing HR function by drawing on the best practices worldwide. The Appendices provide a tried-and-tested HR audit tool, a comprehensive list of HRD competencies and a real-life example of strategic human resources, which should also help focus your own thinking and actions.

If you already run a brilliant HR function, prepare to have your ideas acknowledged and copper-fastened. If you are struggling with the role or simply underperforming, this book should offer a potential jump-start to your efforts. If you are completely new to the role, it will provide a set of 'handrails' to help you get started. A key point is that you do not have to work through each of the 'steps'[7] in the model presented on page xv, since it represents a coherent way to think about the function rather than a 'must-do' building sequence. It is certainly possible to skip some of the individual steps, depending on where you are starting from! Yet by working through the model you can ensure that you build a powerful, turbo-charged HR function. Why should you settle for anything less? Future HR managers, I am convinced, will take their rightful place at the 'top table' without apology. This book will provide them with many of the essential tools.

References

1   See, for example, Jeffrey Pfeffer, *Competitive Advantage through People* (Boston Mass, Harvard Business School Press, 1994) and Randy Schwell, 'Repositioning the human resource function: transformation or demise', *The Academy of Management Executive*, 1990, Volume 4, Number 3, pp.49–60.

2   The Institute of Directors has recorded a movement from 55 per cent to 72 per cent in HR representation at board level in their most recent research (*People Management*, 29 July 1999, p.15). However, there is some contradictory research. The latest results from a survey carried out by

the Cranfield School of Management shows that the function has no more representation at board level than at the start of the 1990s (*People Management*, 25 November 1999). Overall, the picture on this is less than 100-percent clear.

3   Paddy Feeney, Orion International Executive Search and Selection, 1997–2000 analysis period.

4   Source: CIPD Registrar of Members in Ireland 1999. This UK body has over 1,900 members in Ireland.

5   *A Chartered Institute for the Next Millennium*, 1999, page 3. In February 2000 it was announced by the Privy Council in the UK that the IPD had been granted Chartered Institute status. This was effected on 1 July 2000.

6   In the words of Lynda Gratton of the London School of Economics, 'They have understood that what makes great companies is not only the elegance of strategic plans, but the ability to turn the rhetoric into reality' (*Personnel Management*, 16 December 1999, p.25).

7   The nine-step model is meant to be illustrative, rather than a prescriptive sequence. For example, it could be argued that you need to understand the business strategy/requirements (Step 2) before you can 'lock-in' to a specific HR role (Step 1). In reality, many of the issues highlighted have to be addressed in parallel. The sequencing outlined is reasonably logical and should aid understanding.

BUILDING A POWERFUL HR FUNCTION: THE NINE STEPS

Step 1: Mission definition
Do we have a defined
HR sense of purpose?

Step 2: Business alignment
Are we 'in sync' with the business strategy?

Step 3: Functional expertise
What are our current strengths and capabilities?

Step 4: Role clarity and customer service
What is the perception of value-added
by both line managers and employees?

Step 5: Clever structure/Smart processes
Are we 'designed for success'?

Step 6: Adequate resources
Do we have the credibility and clout
to achieve our mission?

Step 7: Internal marketing
What is our internal 'share of mind'?

Step 8: HR metrics
Can we 'measure' the score?

Step 9: Personal impact
Do *I* have what it takes to be
successful in this game?

1   MISSION DEFINITION[1]

When you chase two rabbits you catch neither.
Chinese proverb

Let's begin with the easy bit. The rationale for 'understanding your mission' is simple. If you are not crystal clear on the role of the HR function, you cannot expect line managers to understand and respect what you do. The discussion and variety of models detailed on the following pages will allow you to explore this topic and come to a conclusion on your exact role.

HR *v* personnel management: what's in a name?

The difference between the terms 'personnel management' and 'human resource management' (HRM) has been debated for some years. Complicating this issue, the two terms are often used interchangeably – ie the 'titles' themselves are not a good guide to the type of work involved. For example 'personnel managers' can be involved in very strategic work while 'HR managers' may simply be ploughing the traditional furrows – albeit under a new label. This confusion has led to a slew of articles based on the premise that HRM is 'old wine in new bottles', 'big hat – no cattle', etc.

While there is no 'absolute' agreement on the definition of either term, I believe that HRM is differentiated from personnel along two key dimensions:

1 *Time dimension* – HRM is focused on a 'leadership' (getting ready for tomorrow) agenda while personnel management has historically been shorter-term (today-focused) or even reactive.

2 *Business alignment* – HRM is much more closely integrated with 'the business', HR managers typically having a much deeper understanding of key organisation challenges. In contrast, 'personnel management' has essentially been seen to be about 'people'. A good example of this was the notion that personnel managers were 'interchangeable' across companies and industries – so that detailed local knowledge about a specific business or industry was perceived as secondary or even somewhat irrelevant. An attempt to capture these points diagrammatically is shown in Figure 1.

Figure 1
PERSONNEL v HUMAN RESOURCE MANAGEMENT

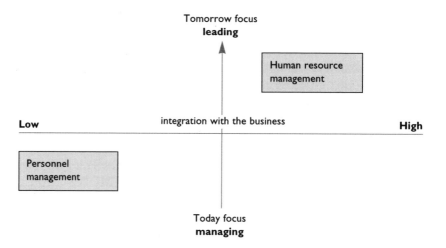

HRM: the increasing 'depth' of involvement in the business

The business alignment argument is clearly demonstrated by the fact that HRM managers are becoming more deeply involved in the business. Human resource professionals increasingly address a wide range of organisational issues – ie the scope of the role has widened dramatically since the days when the personnel function was narrowly labelled 'hire and fire' (see Figure 2).

Figure 2
THE INCREASING SCOPE OF HUMAN RESOURCE MANAGEMENT

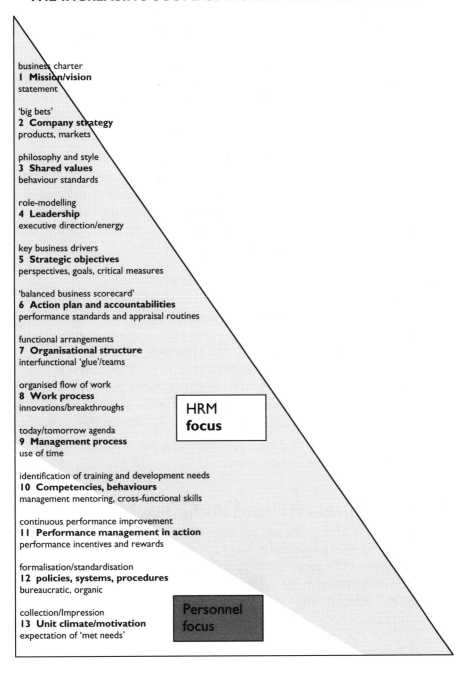

business charter
1 Mission/vision
statement

'big bets'
2 Company strategy
products, markets

philosophy and style
3 Shared values
behaviour standards

role-modelling
4 Leadership
executive direction/energy

key business drivers
5 Strategic objectives
perspectives, goals, critical measures

'balanced business scorecard'
6 Action plan and accountabilities
performance standards and appraisal routines

functional arrangements
7 Organisational structure
interfunctional 'glue'/teams

organised flow of work
8 Work process
innovations/breakthroughs

today/tomorrow agenda
9 Management process
use of time

HRM focus

identification of training and development needs
10 Competencies, behaviours
management mentoring, cross-functional skills

continuous performance improvement
11 Performance management in action
performance incentives and rewards

formalisation/standardisation
12 policies, systems, procedures
bureaucratic, organic

collection/Impression
13 Unit climate/motivation
expectation of 'met needs'

Personnel focus

Over time the historical role of 'personnel managers' has increased in breadth.[2] HR managers now typically operate a wider 'radar screen' and, as a consequence, need a more comprehensive business understanding to contribute fully at the executive team level.[3] Without this depth of business understanding, less successful HR managers are increasingly 'dismissed' by their peers ('We will deal with the soft stuff later') and reduced to wielding the diminished power and influence that accompany this.

The 'progression' of the function and HR managers' role

Another way to conceptualise the changing role of the HR function is to consider its historical progression over time.[4] Although there is no absolute consensus on this, I believe that the HR function has broadly followed the developmental sequence detailed in Figure 3.

The choice is not either/or but among several

You are now entering the grey zone. In reality, successful HR departments often incorporate several of the 'model elements' detailed (see next page); added value may come from implementation of a multi-purpose role. However, the core argument here is that your HR department should have one *predominant* focus – a 'best fit' with your organisations' current stage of development and the specific business issues faced. For example, how would you respond to the following question?

How would you describe the current mission/role of the HR function in your organisation?

Moving ahead: clients set demands for new service levels

Not all HR departments set their own agenda. Although 'being ahead of the posse' may be laudable in some organisations, changes in HR services can result from new expectations set by the line management team, rather than being instigated internally. Recognising the potential lag in orientation, some companies seek to communicate the 'new expectation' directly to their HR troops.

For example, an internal presentation within General

Figure 3
THE HISTORICAL PROGRESSION OF THE HR FUNCTION

Timeline		Personal skills	Business involvement
1 in the distant past	**Administration/welfare model** The role of the personnel department is to handle routine administrative matters/paperwork ('clerk-of-the-works') and to counsel employees **Focus: paternalism and control**	administrative skills empathy	*shallow*
2 in the recent past	**Service model** The mission of HR is the delivery of high-quality services to help recruit, motivate and retain employees HR provide information on request **Focus: responsiveness**	functional expertise	
3 became	**OD model** The functional aim is to *develop* people and promote organisational effectiveness by helping to diagnose line management needs **Focus: development**	organisational theory and internal consulting	
4 is	**Self-sufficiency model** The purpose of HR is to enable people to develop themselves and their organisations **Focus: empowerment**	leadership and wide knowledge of business issues	
5 is moving towards	**Strategic HR model** The function of HR is to become the catalyst for organisational strategy and change (this remains 'frontierland') **Focus: driving transformation and workforce productivity**	being sensitive to the external environment and being a voice for change	*deep*

Electric (*Change at GE: Some lessons learned*) supports the points made above that the expectations of the HR function are markedly different today from even a couple of years ago – see Figure 4.

Figure 4
HR PRIORITY SHIFT

FROM	Changes required	TO
• Specific client services and transactions	Mindset	• Change catalyst
• Fire-fighting		• Business partner
• Meetings and arrangements	Expectations	• Process facilitator
• Recruiting interviews		• Coach
• Personnel statistics	Behaviours	• Productivity consultant
		• Workforce advocate
	Skills	

1980s	Early 21st century

The Ulrich Quadrant Model

In recent times perhaps the best known source on strategic thinking on human resource issues is Professor David Ulrich. Ulrich operates from the School of Business at the University of Michigan in the USA. His 'model' (see Figure 5) is particularly useful in helping to communicate the various components of the HR role and in dividing the work agenda into its 'today' and 'tomorrow' components. It also helps to differentiate between two types of 'customers' (internal managers and internal staff) who often have very different expectations of service. Overall, the Ulrich Model falls into the 'God, I wish I had thought of that' category!

Using the Ulrich Model as a diagnostic tool

In addition to its usefulness in explaining the various components of the HR department's role, the Ulrich model (Figure 5) can also be used as a diagnostic tool to assess *current* HR performance levels. We recently completed an audit of a large public-sector organisation in Ireland, using the Ulrich Model to develop a listing of key issues to be addressed. A summary of the issues presented is detailed in Table 1.

Figure 5
THE ULRICH HR QUADRANT MODEL[5]

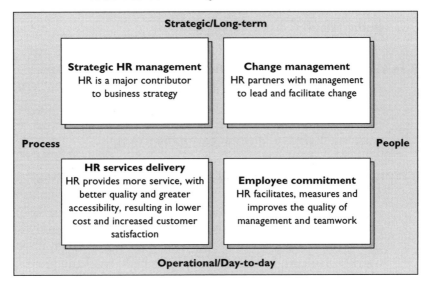

Table 1
ISSUES AT A LARGE PUBLIC-SECTOR ORGANISATION

1 Strategic HR management	2 Change management
• Need for a clear business strategy • Need to align HRM and business plan • Key systems missing – eg performance management • HRM aim-point/goal is unclear • Develop 'organisational learning' mechanism	• Change management 'off-line' – eg change should be conducted by senior team • Partnership/involvement low on current agenda • Sluggish progress being made under a number of headings • Elaborate the organisational values • Manage underperformance • Identify training needs • Develop formal 'scorecard'
3 HR services delivery	**4 Employee commitment**
• Process efficiencies need to be increased • Heavy administration workload • HR system/roles need major overhaul • HR information database is poor • Need to track absenteeism	• Good on training and development • Welfare seen as generally positive • Communications systems weak • Tenure issue needs resolution • Promotions system needs overhaul • Recognition system to be upgraded

Once the client organisation understood the underlying concept, the model allowed us to communicate complex information/diagnostic feedback in a relatively simple way – which is the *raison d'être* of such models.

How is the HR function seen in your organisation?

Another useful way to conceptualise the role of the HR function is to use an appropriate metaphor. In the listing detailed below, I have chosen six metaphors[6] and attempted to illustrate each with a specific company example.

1 Strategist: The creation of a focused organisation strategy

Example: Statoil

June Duffy is HR manager with Statoil, a Norwegian oil company. Statoil, formerly an oil wholesaler, is rapidly becoming a successful retailer, moving into the convenience store market. June and the HR team have been working primarily on 'strategic'-level company issues and then supporting the line management team with implementation.

2 Mentor: Coaching the line management team in 'managing people'

Example: Amdahl

The HR Function in Amdahl, a USA-based mainframe computer manufacturer, was primarily focused on coaching the line management team to manage people really well. Various methods were used to 'engage' the line managers in the creation and delivery of HR policy (*example:* line managers would write 'papers' around new or emerging HR issues and how the organisation should address these within Amdahl). Managing people was a key *line* function. The unspoken philosophy: HR is a support to the line management team, not a substitute for it. Amdahl were universally recognised for their expertise in this area.[7]

3 Talent scout: Sourcing superior talent for the organisation

Example: CRH

CRH are one of the most successful Irish multi-nationals. With more than 30,000 employees worldwide, they have been cited as 'the best-managed building supplies company in the world'.[8] As with all other functions in CRH, human resources management is heavily decentralised. For example, employee relations are handled on an operating company-by-company basis with no reference to 'the centre'. Sitting at the centre HQ (in Belgrade Castle, Dublin) is the HR director, Jack Golden. Jack's primary role is to identify external leadership talent and to nurture/grow existing talent internally. While he also has some minor support duties – talent scouting is the central purpose of his job – CRH had recognised and been fighting the 'war for talent' long before McKinsey's coined the phrase.

4 Architect: The design and alignment of the organisational structure

Example: Black & Decker

Black & Decker have set up a 'Shared-Services Centre' to handle all the accounting work completed in Europe. The rationale is simple. In organisations that have operations across many different countries there is often duplication in 'back-office' work (eg financial control, customer service). Where such work can be centralised, the result is lower costs and higher service levels.

As part of the start-up arrangements Black & Decker hired accountants with second European language skills. This group was sent to several European countries to learn the local processes and to 'import' these into the Shared-Services Centre. Clare O'Hagan, the senior human resources professional, has been leading the design of this structure and ensuring its on-the-ground implementation.

5 Co-ordinator: Ensuring consistency of operations in an auditing role

Example: An Garda Síochána

The HR function in An Garda Síochána (the Irish Police force) is titled 'B Branch'. Historically its role encompasses three separate elements:

- transfers
- discipline
- promotions.

The role of 'B Branch' is to ensure consistency across the more than 11,000 gardaí in these three key areas. While there are 'degrees of difference' around managing in all large organisations, the function of a 'co-ordinator-type' HR department is to minimise differences and ensure consistency in the way people are managed – regardless of their 'level' in the organisation or the location of their posting.

6 Champion: *The active sale/internal marketing of a particular idea*

Example: Sterling Winthrop

As part of a worldwide change programme, Sterling Winthrop[9] in the USA developed a strategic planning/performance-tracking mechanism entitled the 'Strategic Framework'. This had a number of separate elements, both 'hardware' (strategy and planning) and 'software' (company values). The role of the HR function was to 'champion' (design, launch and institutionalise) this system across the more than 100 countries in which the company operated.

The 'software' element of the HR role detailed above is quite typical. HR departments are often seen to embody the spirit or values of the organisation – to be the 'keepers of the crown jewels'.[10] This role is made quite explicit in some organisations.

> I well remember my first trip to HP in the USA. During my induction I thought we were going to run through all the usual functional stuff – how the company run recruitment, training, etc. There was very little of that – the whole focus was on the company mission and values and my role in maintaining the integrity of these. There was no ambiguity; this was the predominant role.
>
> Kevin McNamara, former HR manager, Hewlett Packard

Food for thought

Q. *Which 'metaphor' best describes the role that the HR function plays in your organisation? How clear is this role to you and to the line management team?*

'Soft' v 'hard' human resource management

The final point around 'role clarification' is the attempt to differentiate the values that underlie particular human resource management models. In 'soft' human resource management systems the emphasis is primarily placed on the *human* factor (mutuality of the relationship, a holistic view of employees, empowerment, etc). The historical roots here lie in the origins of the function in Quaker business organisations, in work completed by the so-called 'Human Relations School' in the 1940s and later by McGregor/Likert and others in the 1960s and 1970s.

In contrast, 'hard' human resource management (emphasis on the *resource*) stresses the primacy of the organisation's needs (flexible work models, low-cost versatile shiftworking arrangements, managerial control, etc). It follows that the term 'human resource management' can encompass very different philosophies and organisational practices, some of which are diametrically opposed in their orientation. The debate about visible 'practices' which have the same umbrella title ('HR') further fuels the debate and leads to confusion around the topic 'What exactly *is* human resource management?'

The issue of understanding the appropriate HR role is complex but fundamental in trying to build a powerful HR function that adds real business value. If there is confusion in *your* mind about the role, don't expect the line management team to shine light on the issue. The primary responsibility for role clarity is *yours*!

Complete the half-minute HR test

One of the ways to test mission clarity is to ask an HR professional to communicate in 30 seconds the mission/vision/goals of the HR department. Could you do this for *your* HR department? Some real-life examples of the HR role's being 'defined' in this way are listed below.

HR vision statement

Example from Digital Corporation

Develop a work environment which empowers people to fulfil their maximum potential in achieving world-class manufacturing excellence and optimise their capabilities in identifying and securing new revenue-generating business opportunities. We will be viewed as a showpiece for people development and performance.

Example from Intel

Strategic objectives
Evolve human resource products, services and delivery systems to contribute to Intel's long-term competitiveness and success.

Strategies
1 Employees are proud to work in human resources.
2 Utilise available technology to enable us to do our job better, faster, cheaper.
3 Provide a high-quality staffing service which meets business and employee needs.
4 Foster creating and sustaining the Intel culture.
5 Provide compensation and benefits programmes in keeping with our corporate philosophy which ensures our ability to hire, retain and develop our employees.
6 Develop and continuously improve our people and organisation capabilities to accomplish our business goals.

Example from First Active[11]

HR Mission Statement
Our goal is to become the employer of choice in the financial services market in which we compete. To achieve this we will deliver:

For the organisation
❑ demonstrated understanding of the business strategy and how 'our products' align with it
❑ talented flow of people at all organisational levels, the raw material for our future growth
❑ cost-effective HR service with lower pro rata costs than any competitor organisation
❑ catalysts for change, continuous development and learning throughout First Active.

For managers
❑ responsive and high-quality internal customer service

- a conduit for best-practice thinking in relation to managing people
- an expert support role when needed
- strategies to help our line management partners retain their best performers.

For staff
- the opportunity for personal development and growth: we will facilitate staff in building a successful career
- ease of access to career development and personal counselling through a highly visible service
- a guarantee that key human resource issues are continually represented on the management agenda
- the provision of a positive work climate built on a culture of fairness.

For ourselves
- the opportunity to work within a world-class HR function with clear performance targets and measurement
- a professional standard of excellence in everything we do
- the development of a high-performance team which leads by example in the effective management of staff.

How can you develop an HR mission/vision statement?

There are several possible ways to develop a mission for the HR function, and no shortage of consultants happy to assist in the process! The sequence detailed below (the 'zero-in technique') works reasonably well and is relatively straightforward. A somewhat more comprehensive (and complex) method – a 'search conference' – is also briefly described.

The zero-in technique

Step One: Read something/get some formal input on mission/vision statements and the underlying concepts. This will 'even the playing field', and ensure that everyone on the team understands these terms in the same way.

Step Two: Working with the full HR team, ask each person to write down the key words or phrases they would like to see reflected in the mission statement. After five minutes or so go around the room and record each response on a flipchart.

Step Three: When everyone has had an opportunity to see and hear from everyone else, ask them to repeat the exercise – synthesising the inputs, adding new material as appropriate. Again, visibly record each response on a flipchart.

Step Four: Try to get agreement with the group on the key elements/phrases/concepts that should be captured in the mission statement. There may be three to five *key* ideas.

Step Five: You have two sub-options here:
- ❑ If time permits (ie if you have the HR team away for a week in a deserted location) you can write up the full mission statement there and then, once and for all.
- ❑ Ask the best scribes in the group (or two people) to develop a 'working draft' mission statement based on the agreed elements. E-mail the output. Reconvene in a week or so to refine/finalise it.

Running a 'search conference'[12]

The development of an HR mission/workplan can also be addressed using a 'search conference' technique. The length of this meeting, the selection of attendees, etc, are dependent on the specific organisation circumstances. The 'ideal' duration is three days – ie two 'sleep-on-its'. A defining idea here is to get the 'whole system in the room'. In relation to human resources this could mean the HR group, line managers, union representatives (if appropriate) and employees.

A 'search conference' explores three interrelated issues:
1 focus on the past: what are the issues that have led us to this point?
2 focus on the present: external trends *and* owning our own actions (taking responsibility to 'fix' the presenting issues)
3 focus on the future: the creation of an ideal future scenario.

By working through these steps it is usually possible to find common ground among a diverse set of participants – and to construct a set of realistic action plans to move forward.

Why bother?

Is the 'grief' of developing a mission statement worth the effort? A key part of any mission creation exercise is to 'energise' the entire team. In this sense the goal is not simply the construction of a mission statement but the creation of a 'sense of mission' among the HR team. The level of energy/voltage can be kept high if you ensure that the method used to construct the statement is appropriate[13] and that the 'prize' is explicit.

Working with one organisation, we developed the following 'prizes' in relation to constructing their mission statement.

At the organisational level

There is good potential prize for the organisation in terms of business growth. The market potential for products is growing well. The manufacturing sites have the potential to become a key node in worldwide operations. The corollary also holds true. If our businesses underperform, there is no 'technical' reason why the work could not be done elsewhere in the organisation network at lower-cost sites (eg China or India).[14]

At the functional level

At the functional level, a key goal is for the HR team to be seen within the wider business community as a 'leading-edge' organisation. This is both to attract talented individuals and to allow us to 'blue-chip' our own CVs.

At the individual level

At the individual level, the prize for the HR group is to migrate into higher added-value work (problem-solving, internal consulting, business partnership, etc), rather than working merely on 'administration' tasks. There is also significant personal opportunity to contribute to the growth of the international HR network with policies developed locally spreading throughout the organisation like a positive virus.[15] Obvious career opportunities exist (domestically into general management, internationally into global HR positions, etc). The potential ceiling may be limited only by the personal ambition and the capacity for professional growth of the current members of the HR team.

The story so far...

Let's assume that you 'strategically understand' the role of the HR function – and have captured this in a brilliantly worded mission statement, to which all of your team have contributed. Another key task is 'putting it to the test' – eg discovering if this is what the line management team and the business really need from you. Checking the alignment between the business needs and human resource activities is addressed in Chapter 2, to which we now turn our attention.

References

1   'Titles' can get in the way of clear communications. We are using the term 'mission' here; some HR departments use 'vision', others use 'charter'. For a more detailed discussion of these terms, see Paul Mooney, *Developing the High Performance Organisation*, Dublin, Oak Tree Press, 1996.

2   One of the central dilemmas here is denoting the 'personnel profession with any accuracy, for practices differ so much between organisations and individuals. Rather than referring to this qualification throughout, I fear I must oblige the reader to live with some generalisations – which will of course be true to a greater or lesser extent in individual organisations.

3   In a memorable phrase, HR managers were stated to be in need of acquiring 'business mastery' (Dave Ulrich: *Human Resource Champions: The next agenda for adding value and delivering results*. Boston Mass, Harvard Business School, 1997).

4   The term 'progression' refers to a change over time. It does not imply that the later HR focus is automatically superior to the earlier focus. In practice, HR professionals often have to balance the 'strategy' and 'people' domains of the role. Too much 'strategy' can distance the function from the workforce; too much 'people' runs the same risk of the line management team's suffering the loss of influence implied in this.

5   Dave Ulrich., *op. cit.*

6   The six chosen metaphors are listed for illustrative purposes only. This is not an exhaustive listing.

7   Although the Amdahl star no longer shines bright in the business firmament, they were one of the very early 'sophisticated' multi-nationals with regard to people management practices.

8   Source: industry analysts reports quoted in *CRH PLC Annual Report*, 1999.

9   The company has since been sold and now forms part of SmithKline Beecham, Sanofi and Nycomed.

10   This sets the 'bar height' at a stretch for many functions. For example, where the HR department is expected to embody the company values (everything from completing expenses accurately and honestly to enjoying good team-work among the group), it dictates high behavioural standards for those manning the HR fort.

11   An Irish bank.

12   For a full elaboration on this technique see Marvin R. Weisbord and Sandra Janoff, *Future Search*, San Francisco Calif, Berrett-Koehler Publishers, 1995.

13   One result of poorly facilitated mission creation sessions is that managers all too easily become concerned about the time invested and cynical about the overall benefits. Often mission statements receive 'death by the bottom drawer' (from which they never emerge).

14   This 'negative prize' can also be energising. Details have been changed to protect client confidentiality.

15   A key sub-issue here revolves around the percentage of the HR processes that is mandated by your company internationally in relation to that which is based on local design and business needs.

2 BUSINESS ALIGNMENT

If the HR function closed shop for a month, what would be the implications for the business? If the answer is 'not much', you need to seriously question the role you are currently playing in the organisation.

Wally Russell, HR director, Nortel

For many years the argument put forward by people who did not have a clear understanding of how the HR function should contribute to the business was that 'people are people, regardless of the product or service offered'. The argument was based on two fundamental assumptions:

1 The business of HR is people – there is no need to be overly concerned about the actual business. It follows that the HR agenda followed in Lucent Technologies should broadly be the same in McDonalds restaurants, in Great Ormond Street Children's Hospital or in the Battersea Dogs' Home!

2 The job of HR professionals is to 'discover' best practices (through formal study, networking, benchmarking, etc). There is a one-size-fits-all 'best' solution; the HR role is to find and import this into the business.

Both of these assumptions are badly flawed when put under the microscope. Indeed, the historical assumptions about standard human resource management practices can actually be reversed and might usefully be restated as follows:

Central Idea Number 1: The business of HR is the business

We don't want to hire HR people who 'like people'. They are 'pleasers' and get pushed over too easily. If all they want is a

job with people contact, I tell them 'Become a cabdriver.'
Bruce Dern, Vice-President, human resources,
APC Corporation[1]

HR strategies need to be crafted and custom-fit to the particular organisation culture and operating environment; they work best where they are bespoke. The job of the HR professional is to assess the key business needs – sorting the 'critical few' from the 'trivial many' and developing solutions which resolve the central organisation issues. Because of their preoccupation with standard 'people' activities, often HR professionals are unable to provide tailor-made solutions and services for individual organisations. Trying to install 'generic' systems (eg performance management) can actually hinder organisations; much of the effort gets labelled as 'soft stuff' which is seen as irrelevant to the real business needs. In fact, tensions around 'people versus the business' was historically the staple diet for many personnel managers who misunderstood their role. While this is not to suggest that such internal conflicts have gone away, they may have shifted onto a new plane. In the words of Pete Goss, round-the-world sailor, 'the competition is outside the boat' (address to IPD Conference, 1999).

Central Idea Number 2: There are 'best-fit' HR options for particular industries

There are a variety of excellent people management options which can be very different from each other. For example, in some organisations 'people' are critically important to the service offered – eg teaching or consulting. In others people are, in relative terms, a less important component of the success mix – eg process manufacturing.

A second variable is 'industrial profitability'. In industries awash with money (eg pharmaceuticals in former times) there are many more degrees of choice with regard to labour practices than in less profitable (eg clothing manufacturing/ semi-state sector) arenas.

These two dimensions – (a) importance of people in the product/service mix and (b) industry profitability – lead to the notion of 'best-fit' HR solutions for particular organisations (see Figure 6).

Figure 6

HR STRATEGY/BUSINESS ALIGNMENT – CHOOSING THE 'BEST FIT'

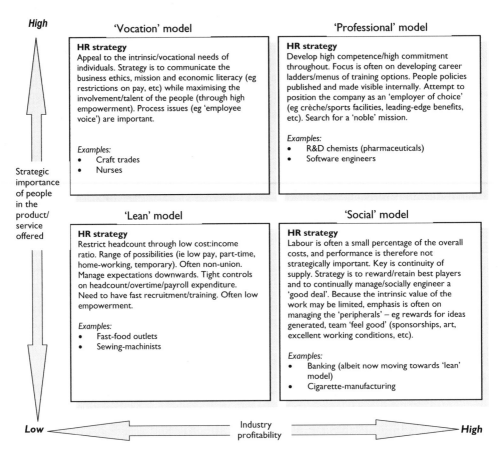

High

Strategic
importance
of people
in the
product/
service
offered

Low

Industry
profitability

High

'Vocation' model

HR strategy
Appeal to the intrinsic/vocational needs of
individuals. Strategy is to communicate the
business ethics, mission and economic literacy (eg
restrictions on pay, etc) while maximising the
involvement/talent of the people (through high
empowerment). Process issues (eg 'employee
voice') are important.

Examples:
• Craft trades
• Nurses

'Professional' model

HR strategy
Develop high competence/high commitment
throughout. Focus is often on developing career
ladders/menus of training options. People policies
published and made visible internally. Attempt to
position the company as an 'employer of choice'
(eg crèche/sports facilities, leading-edge benefits,
etc). Search for a 'noble' mission.

Examples:
• R&D chemists (pharmaceuticals)
• Software engineers

'Lean' model

HR strategy
Restrict headcount through low cost:income
ratio. Range of possibilities (ie low pay, part-time,
home-working, temporary). Often non-union.
Manage expectations downwards. Tight controls
on headcount/overtime/payroll expenditure.
Need to have fast recruitment/training. Often low
empowerment.

Examples:
• Fast-food outlets
• Sewing-machinists

'Social' model

HR strategy
Labour is often a small percentage of the overall
costs, and performance is therefore not
strategically important. Key is continuity of
supply. Strategy is to reward/retain best players
and to continually manage/socially engineer a
'good deal'. Because the intrinsic value of the
work may be limited, emphasis is often on
managing the 'peripherals' – eg rewards for ideas
generated, team 'feel good' (sponsorships, art,
excellent working conditions, etc).

Examples:
• Banking (albeit now moving towards 'lean'
  model)
• Cigarette-manufacturing

Individual organisations can exercise degrees of choice

While there are some 'best-fit' elements, there are also degrees
of choice. Individual organisations can choose to reside in a
'non-typical' box. Harrods provides a good example: this organisation promotes service and high-quality goods as a point of
differentiation. Their human resource strategy reflects this in
relation to the efforts made to recruit the best available talent,
in internal training, communications, maintaining salary
levels relative to the competition, etc. One Harrods recruit told
me that she spent 10 days in training *prior* to being 'let loose'

in the store – 10 days' training for a two-month summer placement. However, this has an impact on product pricing, and the organisation loses some potential customers to lower-cost competitor retailers. It is a conscious decision to compete differently.

The central argument here is the importance of customisation.[2] All too often we come across human resource professionals who are busy installing systems which worked well in their previous employment – forgetting the critical need to take account of the *specific* needs in their new jobs.

Competency-based assessment tools are terrific – in some organisations. Executive training and development can add real value – in some organisations. And so on. There are no sacred cows – just an enormous 'toolbox' of HR possibilities which need to be carefully chosen and custom-fit to the particular organisation. The notion of 'one best way' is ludicrous.

Central Idea Number 3: Benchmarking is a means to an end – not an end in itself

The idea that there are no 'off-the-shelf' solutions is not an argument against benchmarking; rather an indication that benchmarked information needs to be customised in a way that fits the particular organisation. In my experience benchmarking visits to external sites are almost always worthwhile; lessons are often learned which enable organisations to move speedily up the learning curve and avoid 'reinventing the wheel'. Benchmarking usually allows line and HR managers to see excellence in practice (which often has a greater impact than just reading about it). Yet when I work with HR directors, few spend much time consciously scouting for new ideas – other than through ad hoc conversations with consultants, brief perusals of the literature or at industry dinners.

Central Idea Number 4: There are some 'generic' questions that all HR teams need to address

While customisation is critically important, you don't have to start with a blank page. Some of the key generic HR questions have already been distilled.[3]

How do we fight and win the war for talent both at the leadership level and throughout the firm? How do we invest in and receive a return on intellectual capital equal to or greater than economic capital? How do we create an organisation with speed that adapts, changes, transforms, and reduces cycle time? How do we facilitate learning by both the individual and the organisation? How do we create value as measured in the short term by investor and cash results and in the longer term by customer and employee value? How do we create a new culture that affects both employee and customer relationships? How do we profitably grow our business? How do we make sure that our aspirations lead to actions that create results?

HR managers and the creation of business strategy

We have argued above that HR activities need to be aligned with the business – ie that they must be directly linked to the specific business strategy. But the question remains open as to how much influence the HR director should *exert* on the business strategy itself. One senior director at Kraft Jacobs Suchard summed up the position in his firm:

> I don't think HR gets factored into the development of business strategies. HR would be involved in our three-year planning, in terms of development, succession planning and so on, but it doesn't determine which way the organisation goes or how the organisation is going to expand into different areas. HR falls out of the business strategy.

One way to conceptualise this is shown in Figure 7.

Figure 7
HR AND BUSINESS STRATEGY LINKAGE

There is no absolute answer to the question posed on whether the HR director should be involved in the creation of business strategy. In some cases, the HR director/department will be heavily involved;[4] in others, they will be one step removed from this – 'responding to' rather than 'co-creating' this. Although the 'future scenario' detailed above is the aspirational point, ensuring that a focused HR plan is solidly built on a foundation of business needs would be a realistic forward movement for many existing HR departments. However, it should be recognised that 'playing in the strategy arena' requires very specific skills.

> To play the strategic partner role effectively, HR professionals must master the theory and practice of forming and implementing strategy. They must be able to engage managers in discussions of vision, values, purpose, and intent. They must help to define fit between organisational activities. They must understand who forms strategy, what form strategy statements should take, and how to turn strategy into action for both the organisation and its employees.
>
> Dave Ulrich, *Human Resource Champions*, 1997

The message is simple. You get invited onto the 'strategy pitch' only if you have the skills to play at that level. There is no automatic entry based on your functional role as head of HR. On the other hand, an organisation's strategy needs to be clear before you can build 'bespoke' HR solutions. A rewarding although slightly tongue-in-cheek way to think this through is to complete the 'strategic clarity quiz' on page 24.

Given the relentless change amid which most of us live, strategy is probably best understood as a continuous refinement process. It is often less an 'event' that seeks to define the future than an ongoing attempt to respond rapidly to the present.

Food for thought

Q. *If you were asked to give a lecture to a group of post-graduate students on 'organisation strategy', how capable would you be? (If the answer is 'not very capable', perhaps you need to skill up in this area.)*

STRATEGIC CLARITY QUIZ[5]

Current strategy	Score (1= seldom, 5 = sometimes, 10 = often)
• There are multiple, competing visions for where my organisation is headed.	
• At strategy meetings, I hear a lot of motherhood statements about 'being the best' or 'having the lowest costs and highest levels of service and quality'.	
• The organisation leaders talk about having multiple 'world-class' functions, reasoning that if we're the best at everything, we'll have the best overall company (also known as the 'Let's be super!' strategy).	
• Our organisation practises 'budgetary socialism', investing time, money and other resources equally across projects, divisions, departments, and so on.	
• Our strategy statements are expressed primarily in financial terms: net earnings, ROI, stock price, and so on.	
• When asked the question 'What does this organisation need to do really well over the next five years?' most employees respond, 'I don't know,' or the answer varies from group to group.	
• Our strategy is recorded in a thick binder, somewhere.	
• Management readily changes its guiding principles. 'We've already done Business Process Re-engineering, Total Quality Management, Principle-Centred Leadership, and High-Performance Teams; this year we're doing Strategy.'	
• After the senior management team devises a new strategy, it is reified, copied to fancy paper, matted, framed, and hung on every conference room wall, but otherwise largely ignored.	
• We tend to follow the strategies set by the industry leader.	
Total:	

What is your immediate HR agenda?

Linkage is an international organisation involved in the organisation of business conferences. For the May 2000 HR Conference in London ('Innovative HR Structures and Strategies') participants were asked to pre-select topics from the following list:

It is a priority for me and/or my department to:	Level of priority
• re-engineer our HR processes/activities	_____
• shift from administration responsibilities to being strategic business partner	_____
• re-skill staff to respond to changing expectations of HR	_____
• implement tools to measure HR strategy	_____
• instigate change and innovation in our HR departments	_____
• outsource certain HR activities	_____
• implement competency-based tools and applications across cultures	_____
• enhance involvement of HR in implementation of mergers and acquisitions	_____
• set up a world-class corporate university	_____
• operate HR processes on a global basis	_____
• learn more about alternative HR delivery models	_____
• define the new role of HR in a knowledge-based organisation	_____
• centralise or decentralise HR processes	_____
• develop business partnerships with line managers	_____
• set up an HR call centre	_____
• implement innovative models for learning	_____
• investigate the future role HR will play within our organisation	_____
• manage global diversity and integration	_____
• create cross-functional teams	_____
• use competencies to align HR with business strategies	_____
• benchmark HR best practices	_____
• implement enhanced performance management processes	_____
• act as a change agent	_____
• link HR activities to business results	_____
• act as a consultant	_____
• implement a model of HR shared services	_____

The sheer diversity in the topics listed and the fact that so few of these topics would have featured on the 'HR radar' for most organisations even a few years ago highlights the importance of aligning your HR products and services with the specific needs of your business. It truly is a moving target!

Human resource management: how do we spend our time?

In the absence of a defined business plan to work towards, HR departments are faced with a bewildering *à la carte* choice of options on where to focus energy (see Figure 8). The best managed HR departments, either overtly or intuitively, focus on the three to five key strategic initiatives which will really make a difference. In essence they:

❏ demonstrate proficiency in all HR practice areas but don't try to maximise everything
❏ prioritise and focus resources in key areas (the 'critical few') which leverage their strategy/theme and which provide real solutions
❏ build commitment to these top priorities throughout the organisation
❏ enhance credibility by institutionalising these themes, by measuring performance results and by making mid-cycle adjustments as necessary.

Linking human resource strategy to business development

One intriguing idea is that different HR 'products' are needed depending on the stage of business development. Sir Leonard Peach, in an address to the Institute of Personnel and Development,[6] made the point that a range of 'generic' HR strategies can be elaborated and that these relate to the 'business lifecycle' – central point: key issues need to be addressed at particular stages of organisational development (see Table 2).

Peach's model is useful in underscoring the general point made earlier that HR strategies need to be 'custom-built'. However, the generic model presented would, by implication, need significant additional diagnostic work before an organisation could refine its HR strategy around the key items suggested.

Table 2
HR LINKED TO THE BUSINESS LIFECYCLE

	Start-up	Growth	Maturity	Decline
Staffing	Key skills	Skills mix	Vitality	Redeploy
Goal-setting	Flexibility	Growth	Efficiency	Costs
Rewards	Salary + equity	Salary + bonus	For efficiency	For cost-saving
Training	As needed	Skill-building	Supervisory	Retraining
Employee relations	Philosophy	Commitment	Involvement	Flexibility

Figure 8
HR'S À LA CARTE MENU – A BEWILDERING CHOICE

A La Carte Menu

Stable IR
Productivity
Organisational development
Safety policies
Organisational structure
Records and computers
Communications
Culture
Information data
Induction
Counselling
Performance management
Operating costs
Employee relations
Personal development
Teamwork and empowerment
Motivation and morale
Flexibility
Personal effectiveness
Mentoring
Change
HR policy
Rationalisation
Absenteeism
Recruitment and selection
Participation and involvement
Quality and continuous improvement
Influencing
Executive development
Trade union relations and negotiation
Training

The bottom line

1 Individual HR practices are a means to an end – not an end in themselves. There is no intrinsic value to any particular HR 'technique'. Everything needs to be considered in terms of fit with the business strategy and impact on business results.

2 There is a need to adopt a 'vital few' approach.

OK, but how do you link your HR practices with specific business needs?

Probably the simplest way to do this is to determine the key drivers in your business over the next 18–36 months. For example, what are the big organisational issues (whether 'opportunities' or 'crocodiles') that need to be managed in your organisation? The key follow-on question is 'Given the big issues list, what are the specific HR products/ requirements to service this organisation?'

The crucial word here is 'customisation'. The process of determining how the HR function needs to align with the business is deceptively simple: see Figure 9.

Figure 9

ALIGNING THE HR FUNCTION WITH THE BUSINESS

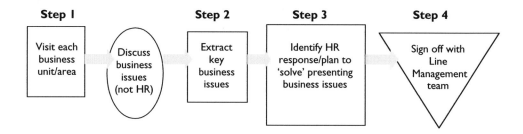

Step 1		Step 2	Step 3	Step 4
Visit each business unit/area	Discuss business issues (not HR)	Extract key business issues	Identify HR response/plan to 'solve' presenting business issues	Sign off with Line Management team

Rolling back the future: understanding the operating context

A clear understanding of the business context (existing and future) within which you will be operating is a necessary baseline for a design of HR systems/processes. To get sight of this,

HR managers need to talk to people within the organisation who have a good understanding of 'what's coming down the tube', and to external consultants, industry observers, etc. Once you have done this, you can decide exactly what HR products/services need to be installed to support the business (see Tables 3 and 4 overleaf for examples of this).

What profile of staff suits our business?

A simple example of HR customisation concerns the 'most suitable' type of work contracts for your industry. Every organisation must address the question 'What profile of staff best suits our particular needs?' and decide the appropriate answer to it. Figure 10 shows this diagrammatically.

Figure 10
SORTING OUT AN APPROPRIATE STAFFING PROFILE

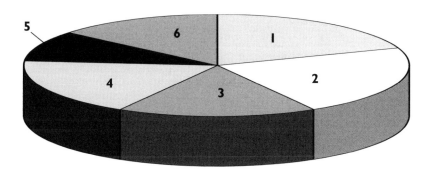

| 1 Temporary |
| 2 Contract |
| 3 Permanent |
| 4 Part-time |
| 5 Home-working |
| 6 Outsourced |

Table 3
HR/BUSINESS ALIGNMENT: MANUFACTURING

List of 'organisation issues' which will affect the business in the next 12 to 18 months[7]	HR imperatives which flow from this – ie a list of key initiatives
1 Cost reduction/higher profitability	Outsource all hiring activity Training in cost analysis/reduction for all staff
2 Business growth in new geographical area (Asia)	Language and culture skills required Cost-effective 'expatriate' programme
3 Hitting sales targets/budget without slippage	Development of business scorecard and internal sales competition
4 New business channel (e-commerce) for sourcing	Finalise e-commerce strategy and publicise internally
5 New product released (upgraded database)	Upskilling on product knowledge
6 Restructuring/downsizing of European operation	Cost-effective headcount reductions
7 Higher productivity per employee	Clarity of objectives and new performance tracking system
8 Improved external customer service	Skills-building in customer empathy New customer service measurement system
9 Increasing product quality	Skilling-up the manufacturing workforce in quality systems
10 New management information system	Programme to support MIS installation and organisation learning processes across all sites
Top 10 business issues identified	**HR-tailored responses which flow directly from the central business issues faced**

Once the 'HR imperatives' have been decided it is a relatively simple matter to place these into a 'normal' project planning format (with specific measures, dates, ownership assigned, etc) which will allow you to 'close out' on these.

Creative HR solutions to organisation problems

Lucent Technologies run a manufacturing/fulfilment site in Ireland. John Barrett is the HR director. The organisation is faced with a classic conundrum. They need a flexible workforce – one that can meet the peaks in demand for the product but who may have no work during 'off' times. The work itself is complex, and product quality standards require a skilled input.

Table 4
HR/BUSINESS ALIGNMENT: SOFTWARE DEVELOPMENT

List of 'organisation issues' which will affect the business in the next 12 to 18 months[7]	HR imperatives which flow from this
1 **Early product obsolescence** As product lifecycles accelerate, we need the ability to develop software faster and bring new product introductions on stream.	• Flexible employees/work patterns – eg telecommuting • Fast recruitment Absorption of new staff into the organisation culture
2 **Proliferation of new products** The future will be characterised by an upsurge in the products brought to market – and a divergence in the type of products with more and more localisation.	• Acquiring the best software talent available • Avoiding undesired turnover of employees
3 **Multi-functional integration** The technical complexity of our products necessitates full co-operation of separate disciplines – ie a team-based work system.	• Temporaries/contractors – ability to use on an 'as needed' basis • Succession planning – to develop and retain our 'fast-trackers'
4 **Project management** The ability to work *rapidly* in teams (which can begin to perform very quickly and then disband post-project) will be a defining organisational characteristic.	• Development programmes – to spread work-load more evenly • Positive discrimination in terms of women
5 **Buoyant labour market** Overcoming a labour market shortage (particularly for technicians, engineers and telesales personnel) will be a key determinant of our success.	• People management culture – fully accepted by the line management team • Leadership effectiveness with an ability to integrate change
6 **People flows** Immigration/settling-in process for people settling back into Ireland. Repatriation back to countries of origin as Irish workforce becomes skilled.	• Good compensation and benefits practices which reinforce the desired culture • Scorecard of key HR metrics for the line managers and the HR group.

However, at the time of writing the jobs market is buoyant and people will not 'hang around' for a phone call from any particular organisation. The solution: John Barrett and the HR team have managed to create a 'Lucent Flexiforce' – a pool of skilled people who have the lifestyle/flexibility to ramp up to meet short-term demands (eg college students, some of whom will eventually be offered full-time positions by the organisation when they graduate). It is a terrific example of the HR group's developing a customised solution to a particular organisation problem.

The 'people pool' concept

Many organisations have experimented with the hiring pool concept (see Figure 11). It has to be said, however, that in times of very low unemployment it can be difficult to manage the 'on-hold' category of people (5.2) who have been interviewed but not yet hired.

Figure 11

ESTABLISHING A HIRING POOL

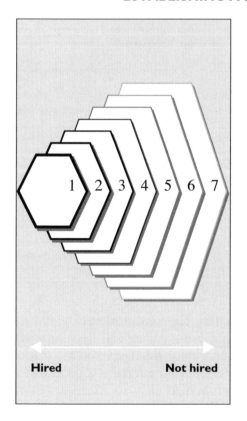

1 Matched employees

2 Mismatched employees
   2.1 who want to move
   2.2 who have to move
   2.3 accelerated development
       programme

3 On call
   3.1 retirees
   3.2 laid-off employees

4 Outside on-call
   4.1 contractors
   4.2 temporaries
   4.3 consultants

5 Outside applicants
   5.1 applicants for whom there is
      a job available
   5.2 attractive applicants for whom
      there is no job available yet
   5.3 high-performing summer interns

6 People we would like to become
   applicants

7 People we do not want to become
   applicants
   7.1 known from prior experience
   7.2 not known

Hired   **Not hired**

Dipped or full headlights – how far forward in time should you focus?

Some of the examples given earlier focus on relatively short-term issues. A key question is whether the HR function should also work on a longer-term organisational change agenda? And the answer is 'It depends.'

There are two separate, yet related, issues under this heading. Firstly there is a need to determine how well the HR function supports the *current* organisation strategy. If the current organisation is struggling to fulfil its mandate, there is little point in developing a 'Year 3000' HR plan. In this sense the delivery of the 'today' agenda provides a legitimacy to work on longer-term issues. However, once this baseline is in place you also need to determine how well the HR function supports the 'future' business strategy. In organisations where the future strategy is uncertain the HR role may become one of 'fog clearance' – helping to determine the way forward. Indeed, the strategic process in most organisations could easily be 'owned' by astute HR managers, who often have the process skills to pull the information and the people 'into one place'.

In practice it is very difficult to develop a fully integrated set of HR actions if the business strategy is not firmed up. Yet in many organisations the strategic picture remains shrouded in a semi-permanent fog – particularly in rapidly-changing environments. The goal is therefore to latch on to as many clues as possible from the operating environment and build an HR response to it, recognising that 'there is nothing certain except change' (Heraclitus).

The danger of being (too) customer-led

Should you innovate, or just do as you are told? If the goal is 'to get to the future' (rather than merely to preserve the status quo), the HR function must be more than customer-led.[8] To limit the focus to customers' expectations runs the risk of placing too much emphasis on the yesterday/today agenda and too little on tomorrow. (See Figure 12.) Bottom line: sometimes customers don't know what they don't know! HR is not simply a customer service function (ie reacting to requests for service); you also need to provide functional leadership to the line management team.

Figure 12

SPOTTING THE CUSTOMER NEEDS OF THE FUTURE

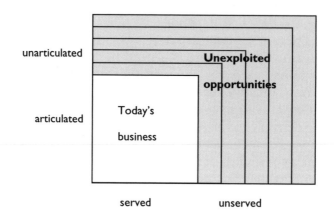

We can use an analogy here with information technology (IT). In an organisation that sells power tools to individual customers, the IT manager may propose a new database which anticipates the 'life usage' of the equipment supplied. At the appropriate time, customers would be contacted with reminders to upgrade their equipment or with information about new products which would fit with their business or lifestyle.

In this example the IT manager is not simply reacting to internal requests for service ('I can't seem to get this printer to work properly – can you fix it?') but is using his or her particular skills to drive the business forward. In similar vein the HR function needs to become a conduit for the very best people management practices that exist – with the proviso, already made, that the suggestions should fit with the specific business needs and organisational culture.

The story so far...

A deep understanding of the industry dynamics and the specific organisation needs provide the bedrock to any excellent HR function. In the words of Albert Einstein, 'A problem well framed is a problem half-solved.' Once this depth of business understanding is in place you can begin to drill down to the details of managing the HR function itself. A good place to begin is to assess the level of functional expertise that exists, and we now turn our attention to this topic.

References

1   Speaking with the author in a seminar on developing the APC HRM function and team, May 1999.

2   A central question to be addressed here is 'To what extent does our organisation need to develop a range of customised products and services, as opposed to using standard available templates (which tend to be more cost-effective)?'

3   Dave Ulrich, *Delivering Results: A new mandate for HR professionals*. Boston Mass, Harvard Business Books, 1998.

4   Based on the personal ability of the HR director, his or her ability to argue for inclusion on the basis of real added value, the culture of the organisation and its HR history, the philosophy of the managing director, management team, etc.

5   D. Ulrich, J. Zenger, N. Smallwood. *Results-Based Leadership*. Boston Mass, Harvard Business Press, 1999.

6   'Human resource strategy and the management of change'. IPD paper, 1992.

7   Both listings of business issues are taken from actual companies. Some details have been changed to protect client identity.

8   This concept is brilliantly articulated in G. Hamel and C. K. Prahalad, *Competing for the Future*. Boston Mass, Harvard Business School, 1996.

3 FUNCTIONAL EXPERTISE

O wad some Power the giftie gie us,
to see oursels as others see us!
Robert Burns

The third element in building a world-class HR function is to assess the level of genuine expertise around the core HR components. There are several different methods to determine the current level of competency/expertise. While each of these approaches covers similar ground, they differ in the 'depth' of the review undertaken.[1] Under this heading there are three central questions to be addressed:

Level 1   How do we *think* we're doing?
Level 2   How *should* we be doing?
Level 3   How are we doing vis-à-vis the competition?

Level 1 analysis: How do we *think* we're doing?

The quickest way to address this question is to hold a discussion within the HR function which should be structured in some way. The simplest way may be to facilitate a discussion around 'What are the things we did really well in the last year?' (see below).

Step One: HR group 'list' their agreed strengths: (real client example)

1   We did a great job in recruitment (by hiring Ms A, Ms B and Mr C).
2   We put a terrific management development system in place with 'X' outcome.

3 We helped clarify the organisation strategy around manufacturing micro-processors in Europe.
4 We 'outplaced' two key underperforming managers.
5 We developed a competencies profile which will assist in
   our future labour intake.

Step Two: Test the data by asking 'How do we know?'

The checklist (Table 5) provides a more structured method to
review the same question ('How do we think we are doing?'). It
can be modified to suit the individual organisation.

Table 5
FUNCTIONAL REVIEW: WHERE DO WE HAVE MOST ROOM TO IMPROVE? (AND WHY?)

		Poor					Terrific	
1	**External: credibility/clout**							
1.1	Understanding the business needs	1	2	3	4	5	6	7
1.2	Having the budget to get the work done	1	2	3	4	5	6	7
1.3	Enjoying high impact/credibility with line managers	1	2	3	4	5	6	7
1.4	Giving great internal customer service	1	2	3	4	5	6	7
2	**Internal: functional expertise**							
2.1	Maximising safety	1	2	3	4	5	6	7
2.2	Recruiting staff	1	2	3	4	5	6	7
2.3	Retaining staff	1	2	3	4	5	6	7
2.4	Providing job security	1	2	3	4	5	6	7
2.5	Training and development	1	2	3	4	5	6	7
2.6	Maximising employee communications systems	1	2	3	4	5	6	7
2.7	Optimising the company way/culture	1	2	3	4	5	6	7
2.8	Maximising organisation flexibility/speed of response	1	2	3	4	5	6	7
2.9	Maintaining positive employee relations/non-union	1	2	3	4	5	6	7
2.10	Monitoring performance control/underperformance	1	2	3	4	5	6	7
2.11	Monitoring grievance/problem-solving structures	1	2	3	4	5	6	7
2.12	Monitoring salaries	1	2	3	4	5	6	7
2.13	Monitoring benefits/non-monetary compensation	1	2	3	4	5	6	7
2.14	Encouraging sports and social activities	1	2	3	4	5	6	7
2.15	Supporting community relations profile	1	2	3	4	5	6	7
2.16	Ensuring organisation's leadership development	1	2	3	4	5	6	7
3	**Visioning for tomorrow**							
3.1	How well do we anticipate the future?	1	2	3	4	5	6	7
3.2	What is the level of external benchmarking undertaken?	1	2	3	4	5	6	7
3.3	Are we involved in the strategic discussions?	1	2	3	4	5	6	7
3.4	Do we have a credible long-term organisation plan?	1	2	3	4	5	6	7

Each member of the HR team completes the checklist. The results are then tabulated and a discussion held to tease out the ratings made. Well facilitated (either by the HR director or an outside consultant), this can very quickly provide a brutally honest snapshot of the function. At the end of it a 'going forward' plan is developed.

Level 2 analysis: How *should* we be doing?

Conduct a full HR audit

When working with GE in the late 1980s I was always impressed by the International Financial Auditing Group. Young auditors (often mid-twenties) would arrive, work for four or five long days, and then present a 'snapshot' of the financial health of the plant. If accountants could do it, could HR professionals? From this early idea I developed an auditing tool – reproduced at the back of this book as Appendix A – which provides a general overview of HR systems (IR, recruitment, training, etc). It should usually be completed by the general manager or HR director of a specific site, and is designed to ensure that:

❑ current HR practices are consistent throughout the company and congruent with the corporate mission
❑ they succeed in fulfilling their stated purpose (eg that training and development are producing actual behavioural changes)
❑ the managerial team is functioning efficiently.

Once the audit has been carried out, the findings and any recommendations (with clear time-scales) should be presented to the senior management group. My sample document (in Appendix A) may need to be tailored to specific circumstances or updated to incorporate the latest thinking on HRM, but it should nonetheless help focus your analysis and save you from the 'tyranny of the blank page'.

Most consultants specialising in this area and the main employer bodies have also developed audit questionnaires. However, the key to success in this area is to work with a high-calibre auditor. Possession of a spirit-level does not automatically make someone a bricklayer. The tool needs to be in the hands of a skilled practitioner.

Typically, what is in and what is out of the audit focus?

The area of human resource management is fairly broad, and there is no 'one best way' to conduct an audit of practices. Furthermore, the depth of the analysis carried out is dictated by individual organisational requirements. Some companies set boundaries that are influenced by the traditional notion of HR management – eg a core focus on the creation of a highly competent, committed workforce. Others wish to encompass a broader approach to HR – eg that the function should play a key role in strategy formulation and organisational effectiveness. If this latter view is taken, the audit would look at such issues as the creation of a focused strategy, primarily through clearly articulated mission, vision and values statements and the human resources role in defining and internally marketing these. It might also include the HR role in creating a 'smart' organisation (job designs that ensure maximum performance, the use of technology to enhance empowerment, etc). The breadth of the audit is therefore dependent on the individual organisation requirements.

Level 3 analysis: How are we doing vis-à-vis the competition?

Benchmarking

The final level of analysis is to review your HR function in relation to best competitive practices. You can conduct benchmark visits to relevant competitor companies to see how some of your practices stack up against theirs. Alternatively, you can take a 'best-in-class' approach and visit some of the leading HR practitioners in any industry. One of our clients in the food retail sector visited Disneyworld in Florida to see how the value of 'making customers happy' is inculcated into Disney staff. While the trip became the subject of a degree of 'good-natured' banter at the time (featuring pointed remarks about a 'free holiday'), the group picked up on three important lessons they were later able to implement across the retail group.

There are a range of technical benchmarking issues to be considered here, although they are outside the scope of this book.[2] One useful way to tap into benchmarking data is to join with associated members of the same industry. For example, in September 1999 the consulting company KPMG established a 'Best Practices Club' for shared services companies. For an annual membership fee of £5,000, companies could attend regular meetings to 'swap notes on executive development, salaries, grant aid', etc. Many similar industry associations have been established directly by companies looking to cross-pollinate their thinking and exchanging good ideas with benchmark organisations. The various monthly and annual CIPD forums provide an obvious source of data for HR professionals who have the energy to pursue this.

The story so far...

Audit mechanisms offer any HR department the tools to review the current level of functional expertise. Audits highlight those areas that are positive and need to be reinforced. They also enable organisations to identify areas of skills in which gaps need to be plugged. However, being expert in a 'competence' sense is simply one element of the success jigsaw. You have to deploy that expertise on behalf of a customer who values the service. In many ways excellent customer service is a combination of both art and science. It is to this area that we now turn the spotlight.

References

1   There are probably a number of additional ways to 'cut the deck'. We have limited the options presented to provide merely a flavour of the methods that can be used to take the HR function forward. This section should also be considered in parallel with collecting data from HR customers. A discussion on this is outlined in the next chapter.

2   For a good discussion on benchmarking see *The Benchmarking Book* by Michael J. Spendolini, New York, Amacom, 1992. See also John Bramham's *Benchmarking for People Managers*, London, IPD, 1997.

4 ROLE CLARITY AND CUSTOMER SERVICE

Better to sink beneath the shock
than moulder piecemeal on the rock.
Byron

The esteem in which the internal receivers of services hold the HR function is a useful indicator of the level of effectiveness. The eventual goal is to design a system that will deliver a level of service that exceeds the customers' requests and expectations.

Assessing the level of internal customer service provided[1]

Under this heading there are six key questions to be addressed:

❑ What do the internal customers want from the HR function?[2]

❑ How do you know? (Is your information simply anecdotal, or have you quantified it in any way?)

❑ What is their opinion of the service provided to date?

❑ What remedial actions do you need to take to satisfy your customers' immediate needs?

❑ Can you design a system that will deliver a level of service that exceeds the internal customers' requests and expectations?[3]

❑ How can you provide functional leadership by going beyond service levels (ie by demonstrating that sometimes customers 'don't know what they don't know')?

How should you determine the level of customer service provided? There are many options, the best of which are explored below:

1 active listening
2 standard consulting questions
3 an internal customer survey
4 using an external consultant
5 the customer-window model.

Option 1: active listening

Probably the simplest way to determine their needs is to engage in 'active listening' with internal customers (ie to listen to what are they telling you they want). However, this approach has a number of potential downsides, not least that waiting for feedback is often uncertain of any result – witness the number of people who, if unhappy, simply do not return to restaurants or stores. While not a perfect analogy with internal customer service, where the audience is more 'captive', that highlights both the social awkwardness of feedback and its unreliability as a stand-alone information source. It is usually best to combine active listening with some of the other methods detailed below.

Option 2: standard consulting questions

Taking positive action, you could arrive at your customer's office armed with a blank A4 notepad and the three standard internal consulting questions:

- ❑ In relation to our current offerings, how do you feel that we could go forward?
- ❑ What do you *not* like that we could amend/improve?
- ❑ What's not happening at all that we need to kickstart?

While simple, these questions should elicit enough data for you to begin to rebuild your HR services.

Option 3: an internal customer survey with the line management team

A useful method here is to ask each (HR and line management) group to complete the following exercise by writing down:

1 the things we believe we currently do well
2 the things we believe we could improve on

3 the things we believe other departments do well
4 the things we believe they could improve on
5 the things we believe they have got on their list
6 the things we believe we could *stop* doing
7 the things we believe they could stop doing.

Another, more formal, method to review the existing HR function is to complete a diagnostic exercise on what your internal customers actually want (see Table 6). This is distributed by the HR team, and the results are tabulated and fed back to line managers – along with an appropriate response.

The data from this survey can lead to the construction of a 'HR improvements priority matrix' (see Figure 13).

Option 4: using an external consultant

A fourth way of monitoring the HR function is to engage an outside consultant to complete a formal review. The basic

Figure 13

HR IMPROVEMENTS/PRIORITY MATRIX

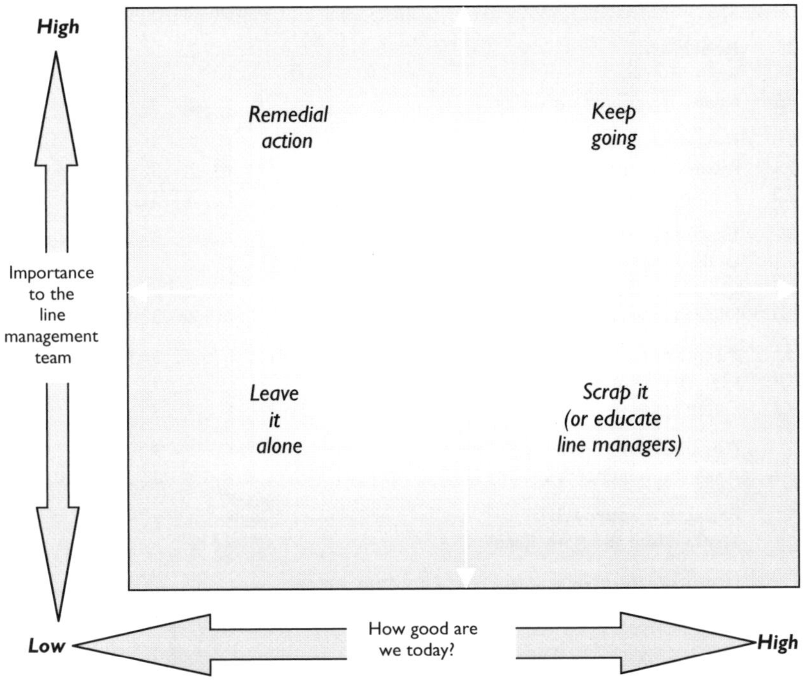

Table 6
INTERNAL CUSTOMER SURVEY

	A: Please rate the following services	How important is this issue for you? Not important — Very important	Rate the current level of service Poor — Excellent
1	Advice you receive on HR policy	1 2 3 4 5	1 2 3 4 5
2	Advice on remuneration packages	1 2 3 4 5	1 2 3 4 5
3	Selection/transfers process	1 2 3 4 5	1 2 3 4 5
4	Recruitment/placement of permanent staff	1 2 3 4 5	1 2 3 4 5
5	Temporary staff	1 2 3 4 5	1 2 3 4 5
6	Summer students	1 2 3 4 5	1 2 3 4 5
7	Advice/preparation of employment contacts	1 2 3 4 5	1 2 3 4 5
8	Staff benefits processing	1 2 3 4 5	1 2 3 4 5
9	Manpower planning/tracking	1 2 3 4 5	1 2 3 4 5
10	Counselling of staff	1 2 3 4 5	1 2 3 4 5
11	Support in staff relations issues (eg grievance and disciplinary)	1 2 3 4 5	1 2 3 4 5
12	Performance review processing, analysis, administration	1 2 3 4 5	1 2 3 4 5
13	Personal development planning	1 2 3 4 5	1 2 3 4 5
14	Input into staff training development (support/advice/delivery)	1 2 3 4 5	1 2 3 4 5
15	Succession planning/job rotation	1 2 3 4 5	1 2 3 4 5

	B: Please rate the following services attributes	How important is this issue for you? Not important — Very important	Rate the current level of service Poor — Excellent
1	**Reliability**	1 2 3 4 5	1 2 3 4 5
1.1	Right first time	1 2 3 4 5	1 2 3 4 5
1.2	Keeps promise on agreed times	1 2 3 4 5	1 2 3 4 5
2	**Responsiveness**	1 2 3 4 5	1 2 3 4 5
2.1	Always willing to help/courteous	1 2 3 4 5	1 2 3 4 5
2.2	Prompt service delivery	1 2 3 4 5	1 2 3 4 5
3	**Empathy**	1 2 3 4 5	1 2 3 4 5
3.1	Understands your needs	1 2 3 4 5	1 2 3 4 5
3.2	Customer needs take priority over internal activities	1 2 3 4 5	1 2 3 4 5
3.3	Shows real interest in solving problems	1 2 3 4 5	1 2 3 4 5
4	**Assurance**	1 2 3 4 5	1 2 3 4 5
4.1	I can rely on information given	1 2 3 4 5	1 2 3 4 5
4.2	Depth of technical knowledge	1 2 3 4 5	1 2 3 4 5
5	**Accessibility**	1 2 3 4 5	1 2 3 4 5
5.1	Available when needed	1 2 3 4 5	1 2 3 4 5
6	**Proactive approach**	1 2 3 4 5	1 2 3 4 5
6.1	Thinks ahead about my needs	1 2 3 4 5	1 2 3 4 5

Please give any suggestions you feel would improve our service to you:

....

....

Add any further comments you may wish to make:

....

....

methods highlighted earlier are available to an external consultant. The same arguments for using an external consultant apply as in any business area (wide benchmarking exposure, expertise in use of methods, no bias, higher acceptance by the line management team on the basis of objectivity, etc). Properly run, an external audit can provide a useful analysis of how the function is performing. The assessment should provide a detailed listing of 'areas for improvement' which can be pursued by the management team to achieve operational or strategic improvements. In addition to highlighting any gaps in the current operation of the human resources function, it could also provide a blueprint for the future.[4]

Option 5: the customer-window model

The final 'structured' way to capture customer feedback is to use the customer-window model (see Figures 14 and 15 overleaf). It helps you to focus on two key dimensions:

❑ the items your customer wants and does not want
❑ the items your customer gets and does not get.

Using these, an HR team can plot the *existing* customer service and also indicate the areas in which there will be most value for you in focusing your time in the future.

The customer-window model is useful in allowing the HR department to do some advance work on the issue of customer service before meeting the customer. (Sometimes when you produce a blank flipchart and ask 'Tell me about our service', the groans from the line management team are audible.) In addition to providing some structure around the discussion, it forces the HR manager (and the line management customer) to assess what they really want from the relationship – ie to formally contract about expected outcomes. As with each of these suggested methods, the HR group ought subsequently to focus on resolving the priority issues highlighted by the line management team.

What do you do with the data?

Once the data is collected it would normally be charted to provide a profile (pluses and minuses) of the current service

Figure 14
CUSTOMER-WINDOW MODEL

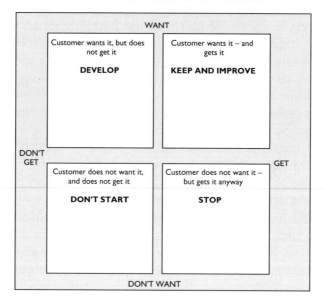

Figure 15
CUSTOMER-WINDOW MODEL 'EXPLODED'

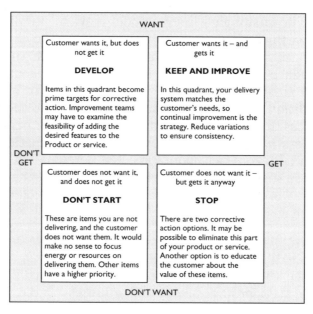

offered. The points listed in Table 7 are based on an actual client survey.

Once the issues are agreed, it is a relatively simple process to convert these into a realistic action plan and subsequently 'close out'.

Role clarity: who owns what?

In some cases the HR activities owned by the HR function are self-evident (eg the initial design of a new succession planning system). In other cases the responsibility may lie 100-per-cent with the line management (eg verbal recognition of work well done with staff). There are also areas where the ownership issues may be somewhat grey (eg formal discipline/corrective action with an underperformer).

Central point: technically there is no absolute split between HR and line management responsibilities – it is a matter for role negotiation in each individual organisation. On the principle that 'people don't resist their own ideas', it is usually wise to pull the line management group into the planning loop at an early stage in this. An example of a 'negotiated' role-clarity (HR *v* line management) exercise is detailed in Table 8.

Internal customer service: the employee as client

Up to this point we have addressed internal customer service in relation to the line management team. An extension of this

Table 7
SAMPLE PROFILE OF CURRENT SERVICE

Current positives	Major HR deficiencies
• Talented group hired with growth capacity • Professional training excellent • IR/ER very stable • Influence change/HR group have clout • Informality/approachability • Technical knowledge excellent • Administration efficiency first class	• Too 'interrupt'-driven: need to become 'more planful' • Calendar of HR events needed • Poor internal communications • Lack of performance metrics • Lack of salary grade/positioning clarity • 'Old' reward system – not reinforcing new message (sales, sales, sales) • Some personality differences HR *v* the line: need to be resolved

Table 8
ROLE CLARIFICATION: HR VERSUS LINE MANAGEMENT

Roles of human resources	Roles of every manager
• Develop HR policies and programmes that meet existing and emerging business needs. • Provide consulting on technical areas of employee relations/legislation. Help managers with issue resolution. • Directly manage centralised administrative services.	• Implement and enforce all HR policies. Monitor compliance, review major expectation with HR. • Resolve people-related issues. Balance business needs and employee perspective. • Effectively execute developed administrative processes.

is to see employees as 'internal customers' who also require particular services.

Viewing employees as clients poses one conceptual dilemma that has to be overcome. At times, the role of the HR manager may put him or her in the position of opposing the 'customer's' wishes (eg where an increase in pay or benefits is sought or in a demarcation dispute). Indeed, the view that the HR function is too closely aligned with the people in an organisation is, arguably, part of the reason for the role confusion detailed earlier.[5] However, with this caveat in mind, seeing employees as internal customers is quite useful.

What are you 'selling' to staff?

There is an implicit deal between the individual and the organisation, from the individual's perspective. The attractiveness of the proposition relative to other options determines who the company can recruit and retain. An attempt to encapsulate this is detailed in Figure 16.

Data collection methods with employees

There are various data collection methods that can be used with employees.[6] The six most useful methods are:

1: Informal, ad hoc conversations with employees

'MBWA' (management by wandering around) is the phrase made famous by Hewlett-Packard. It reflects their philosophy of managers' spending time 'on the floor'. When I worked with Sterling Winthrop, my personal target was to spend 30

Figure 16

EMPLOYEE VALUE PROPOSITION

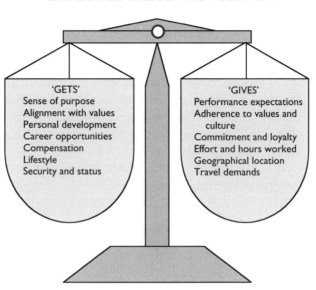

'GETS'
Sense of purpose
Alignment with values
Personal development
Career opportunities
Compensation
Lifestyle
Security and status

'GIVES'
Performance expectations
Adherence to values and
    culture
Commitment and loyalty
Effort and hours worked
Geographical location
Travel demands

minutes of each day in the plant. In this way it was possible to meet a good cross-section of staff and keep up to date on emerging issues. In contrast, a personnel manager at another plant was nicknamed 'Sheila who?',[7] reflecting her lack of fondness for ad hoc conversations with employees or even for moving outside the 'mahogany row' confines of the executive offices.

2: Direct feedback from the line management team

The line management team can be a good source of information – provided it is not the only source you use (because they may tend to hide or be biased on issues). Some HR departments use more structured methods to gather this information (face-to-face visits, weekly 'summary of issues' sheets, etc).

3: Feedback up the communications pipeline

Most organisations have a formal communications system in place (team briefings, 'lunch and learns', etc). Where these are well managed, they can be used as mechanisms to get the employees' voice fed back up the organisation.

4: Direct feedback from trade unions/staff associations

Employee organisations such as unions can be a good alternative source of information. Normally, trade unions are not shy in highlighting issues!

5: Employee opinion surveys

This has become an increasingly sophisticated area in recent years, and there are lots of ways to tap into the thinking of employees. If the other data-gathering mechanisms are in place and working reasonably well, formal staff surveys should not surface any big news. If you do decide to formally pursue this route, it is a very public commitment to following through on the outcomes.

Food for thought
Q. How do you really annoy a group of employees?
A. Ask them what's wrong with the organisation, and then ignore the answers!

Gallup's 12 questions on commitment and motivation of employees[8]

While there are many commercially available survey tools, the 12 questions developed by Gallup have an immediate simplicity which is attractive:

1   Do I know what is expected of me at work?
2   Do I have the materials and equipment I need to do my work right?
3   At work, do I have the opportunity to do what I do best every day?
4   In the last seven days have I received recognition or praise for good work?
5   Does my supervisor, or someone at work, seem to care about me as a person?
6   Is there someone at work who encourages my development?
7   At work, do my opinions seem to count?
8   Does the mission of my company make me feel that my work is important?
9   Are my co-workers committed to doing good-quality work?

10 Do I have a best friend at work?

11 In the last six months have I talked with someone about my progress?

12 At work, have I had opportunities to learn and grow?

6: 'Focus group' meetings with employees, exploring single issues in depth

This technique, as the name implies, helps an organisation focus on specific issues. For example, we have run focus group meetings on topics as diverse as staff retention, sexual harassment and telesales staff motivation while handling routine calls. These meetings allow you to explore issues in depth, moving beyond the 'sound-bite' analysis to really understanding the feelings and perceptions that underpin particular issues.

Engaging the troops: tapping into your workforce and promoting learning

A central role of the HR function is to help develop a competent and committed workforce. The competence issue is addressed through effective hiring and continuous development. The commitment issue is more complex, as the plethora of publications on this issue underscores. In practice I have found six methods that can help to 'up' the commitment level. They all work – to a greater or lesser degree – depending on the individual company circumstances:

- ❏ management by objectives (providing day job role clarity)
- ❏ 'natural' functional teams (using the power of work groups to rework processes)
- ❏ cross-pollination: learning 'across' a company ('one best way' replicated)
- ❏ SWAT teams (high-powered speed teams to resolve key issues)
- ❏ 'bright ideas' suggestion plans (ideas 'drip-fed' into the organisation)
- ❏ 'shake the tree': one-off brainstorming sessions to tap the workforce's thinking.

A brief description of each of these is given in Table 9.

Table 9
ENGAGING THE TROOPS

1 Management by objectives	2 'Natural' (functional) teams	3 Cross-pollination	4 SWAT teams	5 'Bright ideas': suggestion plans	6 'Shake the tree' sessions
Establishment of clear targets/ measurements/ action plans.	Work on process involvement in local area. Goal: Set process targets and improve on them. Mandatory membership. Meet weekly for one hour (or more initially).	Develop 'model' branch office or business process design. 'Pollinate' the organisation with this best practice.	Work on breakthrough projects selected by management. Goal: Put specific 'fixes' in place. Usually selected membership. Either meet weekly or for 1–2-day blitz, as decided by project nature.	Continuous organisation 'trawl' for improvement ideas.	Groups asked to focus on resolving specific issues – eg bureaucracy-busting (removing all non-value-added work in a branch office).
Method System to review these through the annual cycle. Usually includes training element.	**Empowerment** Local management look at all suggested 'fixes' and have decision-making responsibilities for sign-off (up to fix level).	**Method** Various methods. Usually work with pilot/best group. May include external benchmarking. Works well where the result can be replicated.	**Empowerment** Example: budget of £1,000 per project. Minimum bureaucracy over spending this.	**Method** Ideas formally submitted to nominations committee. Acknowledge all ideas.	**Method** Usually brainstorming or nominal group technique. Can be fun.
Inputs 'Forms', buy-in by management team, training, time input into face-to-face meetings.	**Inputs** Training in problem-solving and teamworking skills.	**Inputs** Needs rigorous set-up/design to avoid 'Hawthorne effect'.	**Inputs** Training in problem-solving and teamworking skills.	**Inputs** Needs 'forms', internal marketing and prizes, wall-of-fame winners, etc.	**Inputs** Facilitated event run annually (or so).
Run by Line management team	**Led by** Existing supervisor (who becomes the 'team leader')	**Run/led by** Usually a consultant leads	**Led by** Project team leader (changes from project to project)	**Run by** Internal management or suggestions team	**Led by** Outside consultant or internal manager
Outcomes 1 Clear goalposts 2 Performance feedback/annual appraisal 3 Reward/promotion input 4 Closing of training gaps	**Outcomes** Process targets set/ beaten	**Outcomes** A system that works in the client environment	**Outcomes** Project 'fixes' implemented	**Outcomes** Ideas ranked by 'gatekeeper' mechanism: needs good implementation system to deliver	**Outcomes** List of specific suggestions; ideas need to be ranked by manager; needs to be formally implemented
Fog clearance!	*Let's improve it!*	*A better way!*	*Just do it!*	*Improvement lists!*	*What's possible?*

The story so far...

At this point we shall assume that you've made tremendous progress. You understand the HR mission and have aligned this to the business. You have reviewed your functional expertise and accurately determined how your customers, both line managers and employees, view the service. It's now time to review how you are structured to deliver your mandate. We address this by asking the next question: 'Are we designed for success?'

References

1   Internal customers are defined here as the line management team. While employees can also be seen as internal customers, it is beneficial to separate these two groups because each has distinct needs. This customer service role in relation to employees is covered in some depth later.

2   Who should be involved in data collection? Although the process can be carried out solely by external consultants, my company normally uses an internal manager as partner. This has three significant benefits. Firstly, it ensures that important/complex organisational issues are understood by us as consultants. Secondly, it signals a formal organisational commitment to the project which positively impacts on follow-through once the diagnostic element has been completed. Finally, in a project with extensive data collection and a complex assimilation process, it tends to be very cost-effective.

3   In some organisations these requests may be 'non-traditional'. For example, at Baxter International, Frank LaFasto, vice-president of HR, spends 40 per cent of his time with external customers (eg conducting team-building activities). 'These customer-related HR activities enable Baxter to use HR to meet external customer needs' (*HR Planning*, Volume 17, Number 3, page 3).

4   While outside the scope of this book, there is an emerging organisational development technology that may be of value here. Traditional organisation development essentially focuses on a remedial agenda – the 'gap' between

where the function is *today* and where it needs to move to *tomorrow*. An emerging method called 'appreciative enquiry' (with training programmes run by the National Training Laboratory in the USA) takes a radically different approach – with the emphasis on building on current strengths rather than on shoring up current weaknesses. The two approaches are not complementary, for they are radically different in orientation.

5   In the early 1980s I completed the 12-day management development programme at the Irish Management Institute. One of the lecturers was Frank Scott-Lennon, who runs a successful consultancy business in Ireland. Frank made the argument to the participants that the HR manager was simply the 'line manager who had expertise in the area of managing people'! There was great debate among the participants, with a 50/50 split. Half of the group felt that Frank was right in his assertion; the other 50 per cent felt that the HR manager's core role was to liaise between the management and the staff, a sort of 'managerial shop-steward'. While this point may be clearer now (with more people agreeing with Frank's original assertion), there may also be a hangover to these former ideas of the HR manager as some sort of neutral facilitator.

6   For a full discussion on this see Paul Mooney, *The Effective Consultant*. Dublin, Oak Tree Press, 1998.

7   Name changed to protect confidentiality.

8   These 12 statements are proprietary and copyrighted by the Gallup Organisation, Princeton. For additional information, see M. Buckingham and C. Coffman, *First Break All the Rules: What the world's great managers do differently*. New York, Simon & Schuster, 1999.

5 CLEVER STRUCTURE/ SMART PROCESSES

Our people are too important, too valuable and too capable of doing important work to waste on routine and repetition.
Sinead Brennan, HR manager, Mobileaware

At the top level, HR departments in large (and particularly multinational) organisations are typically structured in one of three ways:

1 Functional structure (recruitment, training, communications, employee benefits, etc)
2 Geographical structure (Europe, USA, Asia, etc)
3 Matrix structure (UK plus Project A; Malaysia plus Project B, etc).

A quick review of each of these, along with the associated advantages and disadvantages of each, is outlined below.

Functional structure: how does it work?

Under this heading the key areas within HR are handled by specialists. A typical structure for a medium-sized organisation (eg 500–750 people) is shown in Figure 17.

The advantages of a functional structure are clear role accountabilities and 'faculty focus' – ie it allows people to specialise in particular areas. The growing complexity of employment legislation for employee relations staff and the huge variety of compensation options for 'reward specialists' are two examples where specialism is becoming increasingly necessary.

Figure 17
A TYPICAL FUNCTIONAL STRUCTURE

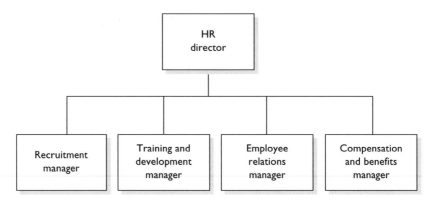

The downsides of this particular structure are the construction of 'vertical walls of inflexibility' between staff in the same department. It can deny development opportunity to people who become stuck in a particular specialism, and may even distance some HR staff from the operating business. Individual specialists can also become disconnected, with the subsequent loss of synergy across the group. Secondary arguments against this structure are the difficulty in sharing the workload evenly, and the boredom factor when a single issue is focused on continuously. However, these potential disadvantages can be overcome by good processes that align the different specialists (the simplest example being a well-managed weekly update meeting). Periodic rotations within the function can also help to overcome any lack-of-opportunity-to-grow issues.

My own war story on this is amusing. (*Now* it is amusing – it was not amusing then.) In 1981 I joined General Electric as a recruitment specialist. We needed to hire 300+ operators for a manufacturing plant. I interviewed literally thousands of candidates, running 8–10 interviews each day, every day, for two years with a break on Friday to check references. My standing line at the time was 'If anyone else, ever again, tells me their school results, I will throw up!' I may have learned a lot about recruitment interviewing, but it was not exactly a happy time.

Geographical structure: how does it work?

The second option for an HR department can be labelled a geographical structure. It can take a number of forms depending on the organisation's size and geographical spread of operations. It might look like Figure 18.

The geographical structure allows HR professionals to become intimate with individual businesses and is often preferred by line managers who have their 'own' HR manager. It can suffer from the jack-of-all-trades syndrome, by which human resource personnel perform general-practitioner rather than specialist roles. It can also lead to a lack of cross-

Figure 18

TWO TYPICAL GEOGRAPHICAL STRUCTURES

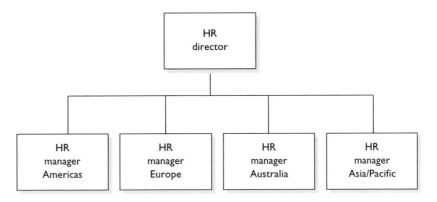

OR – WITHIN A SINGLE COUNTRY –

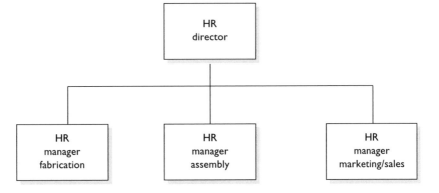

fertilisation across the HR group, and needs good process integration to ensure that HR issues are managed consistently across the organisation (avoiding individual HR managers' declaring independence and developing their own job evaluation – or whatever – systems in a sub-part of the organisation).

Matrix structure: how does it work?

The third structural option is a combination of the two options (functional and geographic) detailed above. A typical hybrid structure is shown in Figure 19.

This structure recognises that within the HR function some roles lend themselves more to a generalist position – eg a personnel officer might be responsible for internal communications *and* monitoring the performance management system. In contrast, compensation is increasingly becoming a specialist area which needs dedicated expertise.

Bottom line: there is no 'one best way' to structure a large or multinational HR function. Rather, there are a number of options with upsides and downsides associated with each, and the call has to be made on a case-by-case basis. In deciding how to structure your department, review the issues detailed in the discussions above to help guide your thinking.

Figure 19
A TYPICAL MATRIX STRUCTURE

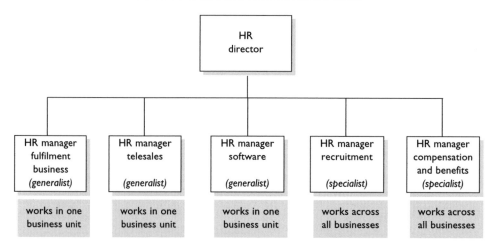

We now move on to the second element of organisational structure – how the various sub-groups within the HR function should work together.

Working on the software: teamworking within the HR function

In addition to the 'hardware' (who reports to whom) you may need also to address the 'software' of the HR function – ie how well the various players operate as a team. While a full review of teamworking options is outside the scope of this book,[1] there are two 'quick' options available, both of which work reasonably well.

HR teambuilding Option 1: round table review

This is a relatively simple option where participants list the pluses and minuses of the current teamwork environment. Using an external facilitator can help to ensure that the meeting stays on track and that no boundaries are crossed without due safety. It allows people to swim to a comfortable depth, while destructive interventions are disallowed.

I vividly remember being involved as a participant in Birmingham. A group of managers from varying backgrounds were exploring the topic of internal consultancy. During one of the group sessions one participant began to touch upon some very deep and troubling personal issues about his relationship with his wife.

After some 20 minutes or so I intervened to say that this person was very much in distress and was bringing up personal issues that were in no way relevant to the theme of the workshop. The facilitator suggested I was 'in denial of my own feelings' and continued the session with the individual until the 5.30 cut-off time. Then she announced 'That's it for today! See you all in the morning!' The individual was left in a very disturbed state.

Team building exercises are analogous to surgery – you should never open up anything that cannot be closed in the same meeting. Business team interventions are not therapy sessions and you need to ensure that people swim to a depth where they are comfortable. Sometimes throwing people in at the deep end results in a condition called drowning!

HR teambuilding Option 2: complete a teamwork checklist[2]

This is still a relatively neutral and 'safe' agenda item in that it is not personalised. Typically, a group would complete the checklist in advance. At the meeting the items listed become the focus of attention. A typical list of issues to be addressed is detailed in Table 10.

Table 10
HR MANAGEMENT TEAM CRITERIA – THE TOP 10 INDICATORS

The top 10 indicators	Issues for us under this heading?
1 Shared/common purpose/clear strategy	
2 Stretch targets: goal of continuously improved performance (with metrics assigned)	
3 Clear understanding of short-term roadblocks (6–12 months)	
4 Performance benchmarks against best-in-class (named) with visible scorecard	
5 Appropriate leadership (includes boundary management with external groups)	
6 Managerial processes that are effective and economical in time usage	
7 Strong, independent career-oriented managers; sense of control over own destiny (not 'schoolchildren')	
8 Robust personal relationships: conflicts can be openly expressed, dealt with. The openness is often tempered with a sense of fun/humour.	
9 Mutual interdependence (notion of internal customer service)	
10 Rewards for excellence	

Smart processes: are we working efficiently?

One way to think about the HR function is that it provides a range of services to the line management team. These HR processes can be mapped and re-engineered – if necessary – to improve the level of internal service.[3] For example, working with one client we mapped the recruitment process and were subsequently able to reduce the lead-time for the recruitment of a mid-level manager from 87 to 40 days (a 54 per cent time-saving).[4]

Smart processes: quicker, cheaper, better

Process re-engineering has had a market impact on the way in which businesses are designed. While most often associated with back-office work in financial services, business process re-engineering has now begun to impact human resource departments in a number of ways.

Objectives under this heading are:

1   to identify the 'products' delivered by the HR department
2   to determine the effectiveness of existing work processes
3   to develop a prioritisation of work processes that need to be redesigned.

Underpinning this is the rapid advancement of information technology, which allows organisations to substitute routine transactions with highly versatile information systems, giving managers and employees direct access to information. This reflects an organisational shift towards empowering employees to make decisions with the use of expert systems. Secondly, the notion of business process redesign has given new life to the old science of industrial engineering or, to express it in simple terms 'working smarter'.

Drilling into the details: what exactly are work processes?

Processes are the structured collection of activities by which an HR department does what is necessary to produce value for its customers. They are measured in terms of customers' satisfaction with the output. The motivation to improve existing processes comes from a need to:

❏   provide enhanced customer service (eg better applicant screening for the business or allowing people instant access to information that they require)
❏   derive greater value from substantial investment in

technology (eg to determine what elements of HR work can be completed on-line)

❑ significantly increase added value or reduce costs

❑ use time as a competitive weapon (condensing cycle time in the key HR processes).

Underlying approach and design rules

Designing new processes involves focusing on the expected outcome and attempting to compress both time and cost. Parallel activities are often linked and integrated (to shorten the cycle time). The trend is to collect information once only and at source. IT can be used as an enabler of smarter process design (eg some of the new tracking software systems in the recruitment/applicant screening areas). However, the trend is not simply driven by an efficiency agenda (doing the same things smarter) but focuses on the effectiveness agenda ('Are we doing the right things?'). 'The focus shifts from throwing lifebelts to drowning people to walking upstream and finding out who is throwing them off the bridge, and why.'[5]

Within the HR function, processes tend to be small and self-contained (ie they tend to be within the control of the HR group). Once the key HR processes have been decided, it is then possible to map them. Normally, processes are composed of three elements:

1 what companies think the process involves (this needs to be mapped for the key processes selected)

2 what the process actually involves (this emerges from the previous step and is often significantly different from what organisations think is in place)

3 a redesign of the process, to save time/effort, provide better customer service, etc.

Business process re-engineering: how this relates to HR departments

To understand the relevance of business process re-engineering we need to consider how HR adds real value (see Figure 20). The attempt is to move away from the 'cost' to the 'added-value' side of the agenda, ensuring that the function is spending time on the issues that will really drive the business forward.

Business process re-engineering example from Intel

That was then...
Intel Ireland employ 2500+ people directly and about 1500 in sub-contract companies at their manufacturing site in Leixlip, Co. Kildare, Ireland. During the start-up phase the HR department in Intel used to distribute performance management forms to managers who needed them. The process was time-consuming. Because of the scale of the operation, on a daily basis dozens of on-site managers would call the HR department for blank forms, often with queries on how the process worked. Managing this process with such a large group took up a considerable amount of time.

This is now...
The HR team redesigned the process. Blank forms are now available on-line to all managers, along with guide notes on how the process works.

The outcome...
This has freed up about one man-year of time annually – time that can more usefully be spent on higher-added-value activity.

Figure 20
HOW HR ADDS REAL VALUE

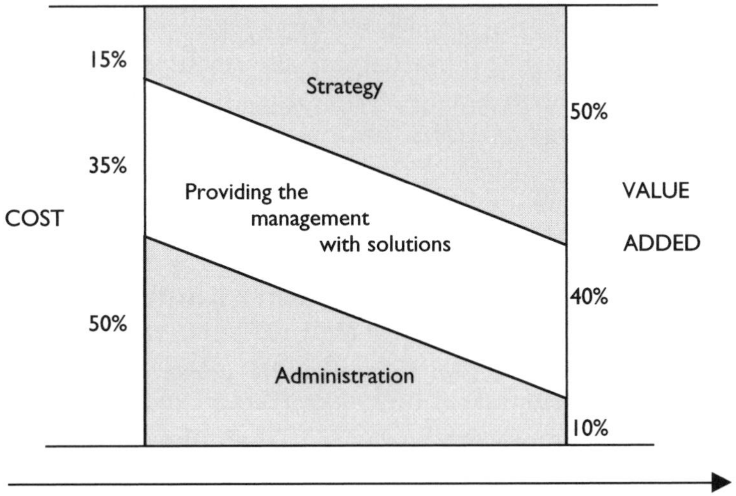

What is the end goal?[6]

As with any internal change project it is useful to begin with the end in mind. The specific goals set will depend on the underlying driver for the project. Is it a cost review ('We need to reduce the cost of the HR function from 'X' to 'Y'), a customer review ('HR must spend more time helping us to solve critical business problems and adding more business value') or an internal HR review ('We need to "stretch and change" or fix some element of poor current performance')? Whatever the underlying motive, the project goal has to be clearly articulated. It could be something along the lines outlined below:

❑ *Project goal 1*

A central HR operation that will meet our customers' ongoing/evolving needs at an acceptable cost.

❑ *Project goal 2*

Creation of the capacity within HR to undertake additional value-added activities without increasing headcount or operating costs.

❑ *Project goal 3*

Installing a self-service system by which management and employees can avail themselves of HR services with a higher degree of autonomy/self-sufficiency.

Moving to a new model of HR/services delivery

In some organisations the strategic context has changed. This has led to the development of new service delivery models for HR departments. Two specific developments are worthy of note:

1 The emergence of e-business has led to the notion of 'e-service' – a sort of 'Internet time' in which normal servicing times are massively compressed. Faster business cycle times demand faster service cycle times.[7] The greater flexibility and agility required of all external service providers is finding its way in-house; the effect is to increase the demand for high-speed, improved quality and lower costs.

2 Employees and potential employees are customers and not passive recipients of services.

There is increasing demand for seamless services (a 'one-stop shop') and for movement towards self-service. The overall effect is a growing need to improve access to information for internal customers of HR. As a result of these pressures, a new model of HR service is emerging. A typical example of this emerging structure is detailed in Figure 21.

Figure 21
THE EMERGING MODEL OF HR SERVICE DELIVERY

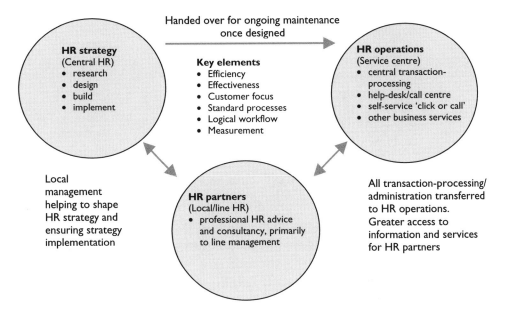

How is this superior to what currently exists?

The emerging pattern of HR organisation design has a number of benefits. An attempt to summarise these is shown in Table 11.

Redesigning your HR processes: some key questions

1: Are our existing processes adding value to the business?

- ❑ Does everything we do make sense?
- ❑ Is everything we do done 'smartly' (eg involving the use of expert IT system)?

Table 11
BENEFITS OF THE EMERGING HR STRUCTURE MODEL

For HR	For line management	For employees	For the organisation
• Clear and simple processes • Automation • Focus on what the customer really wants • Centres of excellence • 'World-class' function	• Easier people processes • Autonomy and accountability for the 'people piece' • Improved HR service • Speed of service	• Consistent communications • One point of contact • Clear and simple HR processes • Quicker turn-around • Access to information	• Better utilisation of resources • Focus on 'individual' element • Flexibility • Measurable HR contribution

2: Are we cost-effective?

❑ Do we benchmark our processes/services?

❑ How do we compare with 'best-in-class'?

3: How do we achieve truly world-class service levels?

❑ What opportunities do we have for centralised transaction processing?

❑ Could we achieve any economies of scale (and if so, where)?

❑ Would standardisation of any processes (eg hiring, performance management) help to eliminate time wastage?

❑ To what extent would integrating processes and/or systems save time/processing expense? Can we make these really seamless?

4: How can we leverage technology?

❑ How do we encourage employees/managers to do more self-service (PC, HR kiosk, phone)?

❑ How can we utilise Web technologies?

❑ Would Lotus Notes or the creation of an intranet add good business value?

❑ What benefits can we derive from SAP or other applications already in place?

5: How can we leverage our existing resources?

❏ To what extent, if any, can we utilise centres of excellence across the world (eg all strategy work completed in the UK; all training design completed in Malaysia)?

6: Where might additional savings be made?

❏ Less hard-copy distribution of materials (eg employee handbooks)?

❏ Achieve growth in self-service (reduced HR cost/staff savings)?

❏ Outsource some admin. functions (eg payroll transaction) at a lower cost?

❏ Reduce cycle time (eg simpler process to manage performance or collect data on training needs)?

❏ Reduce HR headcount?

❏ Reduce administration/transaction costs?

❏ What are the big time-consuming issues at the moment? How could we eliminate them?

7: How do we compare with external agencies?

❏ Should we 'make 'or 'buy'? Would it be possible/beneficial to outsource some of the current services being offered? [8]

Outsourcing elements of the HR function has been common for some years (eg the use of specialist recruitment firms). Areas like recruitment, training and salary/benefits administration seem obvious targets for outsourcing (often referred to as the 'transactional' elements of HR). However, there is a growing body of organisations who are experimenting with the notion of outsourcing huge chunks or even the *entire* HR function. [9]

The use of application service providers (ASPs)

In recent times there has been significant growth in the number of application service providers. These external companies offer organisations a package of IT-based products – system functionality, data storage, reporting tools, helpdesk and maintenance.

Access to such a system is usually through the Internet or an ISDN/modem link. Instead of buying system software, organisations pay a monthly or quarterly fee to the ASP or may arrange to pay a charge for individual transactions.[10]

The advantages of ASPs have been listed as:

- Organisations do not need in-house IT expertise to set up and run their systems. Everything is done by the ASP, including back-ups and upgrades.
- With a minimum requirement of a personal computer and a telephone line, systems can be up and running quickly – suppliers are quoting in weeks rather than months.
- Capital outlay is minimal, while system costs are transferred from capital to revenue (which pleases the accountants).
- ASPs offer software solutions across a range of functions that might not be economical for an individual client to buy – for example, psychometric testing, legal advice and occupational health recording.

At the time of writing, a number of business options are emerging in this area and it would seem that the idea has significant potential in relation to the cost-effective management of the HR function. One of the disadvantages includes the key concern about data security, which needs to be overcome.

In practice, the 'make versus buy' decision can be made against any aspect of human resources, and *should* be made (preferably by the HR professionals themselves, rather than being imposed by the line management team).

The story so far...

You've now defined your role, aligned this with the business, completed a functional audit and run the whole thing past your customers. Phew! You've then aligned your structure and process to deliver on the commitments made. It leads to the next question: 'Do you have sufficient resources to make it happen?'

References

1   For a deeper discussion on this see Paul Mooney, *Developing the High Performance Organisation*, Dublin, Oak Tree Press, 1996.

2   There are myriad 'team effectiveness' checklists available commercially – or you can create your own. The checklist detailed is for illustration purposes only.

3   Often you find fragmented processes – eg manual interventions, excessive paperwork, multiple hand-offs, unnecessary approvals and awkward communications channels. These lengthen cycle times and cause duplication of effort.

4   While this provides a very real example of process re-engineering, it hardly represents 'best practice' in terms of time management. Moyna Noble is the HR manager for the Xerox operation in Blanchardstown, Dublin. Her previous job was in an HR role in San Francisco. While at home in Ireland on Christmas holidays she attended a 'jobs fair' to test the local market. Less than 24 hours later she sat on the return flight to San Francisco with a copy of her formal job offer and contract from Xerox. Good talent is scarce. The best-managed companies recognise this and don't hang around. This is increasingly being recognised – with practices changed to emphasise speed. For example, historically the recruiter (the HR person) was involved in salary negotiations. Many organisations are putting down negotiating authority for entry salaries as a line management function – within pre-established ranges. It follows that line managers can make job offers instantaneously.

5   Nick Georgiades, 'A strategic future for personnel', *Personnel Management*, February 1990, pages 43–6.

6   This has the additional benefit that in a time of scarcity of skilled resources it allows HR professionals to work on higher-value-added activity.

7   The growth in the recognition of speed as a competitive weapon underpins this. For an excellent discussion on this see George Stalk, Jr and Thomas M. Hout, *Competing against Time*, London, The Free Press, 1990.

8   Outsourcing is often cheaper for three reasons: 1) specialist companies are more cost-effective due to the economics of scale; 2) there is no need to provide contractors with employee benefits (after all, the hidden costs of an employee contract can load an additional 40 per cent on top of base costs); and 3) the relationship is transitory and can easily be severed when the work is completed.

There is growing evidence that this argument is gaining more ground (eg BP/Amoco's decision to put out all of its HR administration to EXACT, a new outsourcing enterprise based in California – this is seen by some people as heralding a new trend, the first in a long line of similar contracts). *People Management*, 3 February 2000, page 48.

9   For a good discussion on this see 'Premier division: how Westminster City Council has outsourced the bulk of its personnel function', *People Management*, 19 August 1999, pages 36–41.

10   For a full discussion see 'ASP: As Soon as Possible?' *People Management*, 13 April 2000, page 51.

6   ADEQUATE RESOURCES

The best preparation for tomorrow is to do today's work superbly well.

Sir William Osler

A key determinant of the human resource department performance is often the extent to which the function has adequate resources (manpower, appropriate skills, budgets, political clout within the management structure, etc) to meet its mission. In our experience, a frequent cause of poor HR performance is a lack of investment and resources. The lack of funding leads to a drop in performance and a vicious cycle is established whereby future funding is difficult to obtain. In essence, human resources becomes a Cinderella function – and is *never* invited to the ball!

Rationale: vision needs execution, which in turn requires organisational capability – ie resources. Ensuring adequate resources is therefore a key determinant of the success of HR departments. In practice, there are a number of key questions that must be addressed under this heading:

Q. Who are the key stakeholders?

Q. What authority do we (the HR function) command with these?

Q. What resources do we realistically need to fulfil our mandate?

Grab attention! Proving your worth to the business

In a business world of limited resources, how do we get the money?

The central issue here is similar for all functions – ie proving your worth to the business. One way to prove your worth is to use the available HR 'energy' to focus on some key presenting issues within the organisation. Once diagnosed and successfully resolved, this can provide a powerbase on which to build your case for sufficient resources. It follows that a diagnosis of existing organisation problems can provide a short-term agenda for the HR function which is highly visible. If it is directed at the key decision-makers, your case is half way there!

I have coached a number of new HR managers to negotiate sufficient organisational support as part of their signing-on fee. If this can be done in advance of your entry to an organisation, all the better. However, the size of the mountain to be climbed is often not visible until you have started the climb itself. It follows that the level of organisational support needed may have to be determined *after* you have accepted the appointment.

When a new manager takes charge...

In one client organisation the new HR manager diagnosed the following issues:

1 The mission of the organisation was not clear. This had led to continuous debate around product strategy and the appropriate organisation structure to support it.

2 New product development systems were inadequate/poorly funded. Specifically, there were insufficient resources in place to drive innovation forward. There were also related problems in obtaining capital to overcome this.

3 The 'voice of the customer' was not getting into the operation. The organisation was performing poorly against existing customer metrics and the trend was in decline.

4 There was a need to improve multi-site integration. The current interlinking mechanism between Ireland and the USA was ineffective and significant energy was spent in conflict reduction.

5   There were two key leadership issues which needed to be addressed.

- ❏ The depth of managerial bench strength was weak, with few 'ready now' candidates.
- ❏ The management style/philosophy tended to over-focus on technical issues (most of the senior team were engineers).

Armed with this working diagnosis the HR manager was able to 'grab attention'. She had the organisational skills to resolve the issues highlighted and quickly proved her worth to the business – overcoming the HR budget deficit problem that had dogged the previous incumbent.

How this option would normally be progressed

- ❏ The HR manager would complete a full diagnostic of the operation. This would involve designing a data-collection method (often semi-structured meetings with personnel across international boundaries or within the individual country's sites).[1]
- ❏ From these meetings a diagnostic report/presentation would be developed which would be fed back to the line management team.
- ❏ Assuming that they agree with the analysis, a method to close the gaps would be identified and decided upon.
- ❏ Because there is a limited amount of managerial energy, this would be completed on a prioritised basis – eg 'top 10'.

What is our mission? A 180-degree return to an earlier place

The issue about adequate resourcing goes right back to our earlier examination of 'What is the HR mission?' If even the HR manager is confused about this question, it is almost impossible to sell the function internally. Faced with this confusion some HR managers decide to internally compete on 'zero cost' – 'I will run the tightest ship in this organisation'. They become extremely sensitive about 'spends', and paranoid about budget overruns. Taken to extremes it can lead to HR departments being cash-starved. This *is not* an argument that success equates with the size of the consulting budget. It *is* an argument that every HR manager needs to have sufficient resources (including external consultants appropriately used) to deliver on the mandate. The 'tight ship' school of human resource management provides a Pyrrhic victory – if the longer-term outcome is for the function to underperform.

Are you plying your trade in the right place?

Some years ago I had an initial contact with a large manufacturing organisation. The job was to run a short workshop on the topic of customer service. It had an educational piece at the front end and some working through of the issues during the second half. The workshop was successful – we got through the agenda – emerging with a reasonably well-thought-out and detailed action list. I waited for the follow-through phone calls to get additional work, helping to implement the agreed actions. The call never came.

I rang the client to discuss this. Despite his protestations that everything had gone '100-per-cent', there was no follow-through. Unsure of exactly what had happened, I discussed the case with a colleague (using another consultant in a shadow capacity is often useful to help determine your own role in change projects). We had an amusing conversation which ran like this:

ME	I have had a difficulty with a client and am trying to figure out what exactly went wrong.
COLLEAGUE	OK, tell me what happened.
ME	Well... [I detailed the sequence of events described above.]
COLLEAGUE	Who was the client?
ME	I'd rather not say.
COLLEAGUE	OK – if I can guess who the client is, will you confirm it?
ME (intrigued)	Yes.

He guessed correctly, first pop! It subsequently emerged that this organisation's executives 'don't use consultants', except for short/sharp bursts of theory – the executive team *always* work the implementation themselves, and this was well known within the consulting world (except to me!). I had a good 'product' (project implementation) but was selling it in the wrong place (a client who worked on a 100-per-cent self-sufficiency agenda). In similar vein, are you plying your HR trade in the right place – ie do the line managers fundamentally believe that you are adding business value?

The coming of age of HR management

Some organisations require/mandate that HR thinking gets integrated into business planning. In organisations committed to this, the issue is given serious priority, time and procedures being invested in the process. For example, during my own career with General Electric the active involvement of HR managers in the strategy formulation process was quite evident. Firstly, HR professionals were given training in business strategy to provide them with the tools that allowed them contribute to this debate. Secondly, the strategic planning guidelines included a specific human resources element – which was mandatory. However, while various mechanisms exist to impel HR on to the managerial agenda, the 'seriousness' of the issue is determined by the core line management's belief about whether HR 'adds real business value'!

How it actually works. . .

A central question here is whether the line managers are really sold on the positive impact of the HR function. Have you made the 'treating people well leads to superior performance' economic arguments stick? To what extent can such arguments be justified – ie where is the evidence for it? This equation has been attempted by a number of commentators. For example, Jeffrey Pfeffer[2] argues the causal link between HR and business performance works as shown in Figure 22.

❑ People work harder, because of the increased involvement and commitment that comes from having more control over and say in their work.

❑ People work smarter; high-performance management practices encourage the building of skills and competence and, as importantly, facilitate the efforts to enhance organisational performance.

Figure 22

THE CAUSAL LINK BETWEEN HR AND BUSINESS PERFORMANCE

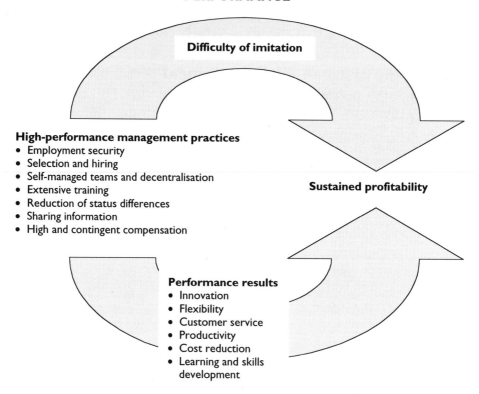

Difficulty of imitation

High-performance management practices
- Employment security
- Selection and hiring
- Self-managed teams and decentralisation
- Extensive training
- Reduction of status differences
- Sharing information
- High and contingent compensation

Sustained profitability

Performance results
- Innovation
- Flexibility
- Customer service
- Productivity
- Cost reduction
- Learning and skills development

❏ High-commitment management practices, by placing more responsibility in the hands of people lower in the organisation hierarchy, save on administrative overheads as well as on other costs associated with having an alienated workforce in an adversarial relationship with management (ie the 'cost of control').

In similar vein, Schuler and MacMillan (*Personnel and Human Resource Management*, West Publishing, 1984) and Lengnick-Hall and Lengnick-Hall (*Interactive Human Resource Management*, Quorum, 1990) posit that a strategic approach to HRM has a number of organisational benefits (increased profits, lower turnover, increased sales, lower costs, increased flexibility, etc). For example, it can be argued that success in employee retention leads to improved business performance (see Figure 23).

Figure 23
THE BENEFITS OF A STRATEGIC APPROACH TO HRM

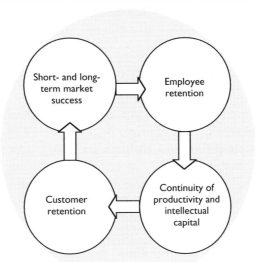

Based on large-scale survey evidence on the HR practices and financial performance of a number of top US companies, Huselid found a strong positive relationship between high-performance work practices and organisation performance:

> Prior work in both the academic and popular press has argued that the use of high-performance work practices will be reflected in better firm performance. This study provides broad evidence in support of these assertions. Across a wider range of industries and firm sizes, I found considerable support for the hypothesis that investments in such practices are associated with lower employee turnover and greater productivity and corporate financial performance.
>
> (Mark Huselid, 'The impact of HRM practices on turnover',
> *Academy Management Journal* 38, 1995)

Overall, there is good support in the literature that a strong, positive relationship exists between high-performance work practices and organisation performance.[3] Perhaps the best-known case put forward is that of the Sears Retail Group. Sears established the 'employee–customer profit chain' which showed that a five-unit increase in employee commitment had led to a 1.3-unit increase in customer satisfaction, and this in turn led to a 0.5 per cent increase in revenue (*Harvard Business*

Review, January–February 1998). This illustrated a clear, predictive link between employee attitudes, customer satisfaction and business results. While many people might have understood this intuitively, the Sears model lent it business measurement and credibility.

Where do conventional financial measures fail?

In his book *Delivering Results: A new mandate for HR professionals* (Boston Mass, HBS Press, 1998), Dave Ulrich illustrates this point brilliantly. While the combined 1996 sales of General Motors and Ford ($300 billion) exceed those of Microsoft, Merck, Intel and Disney by a factor of six, the market capitalisation of this latter group of highly successful creative companies ($320 billion) is over four times larger than that of General Motors and Ford ($80 billion). Microsoft has fixed assets of only $930 million but a market capitalisation of $85 billion, while IBM's asset base exceeds $16 billion but its market capitalisation is only about the same. Much of this difference is to be found in the intellectual capital of these technologically and creatively innovative companies and the skills, competency and motivation of their knowledge workers.

The significance of this for the 'distributed' organisation

The emphasis on managing people well is particularly important for a 'branded distributed company' – one that is geographically dispersed across a large number of separate units or branches, and that projects a strongly-defined brand image of values, service and quality. A retail bank is a good example. Often, large-scale advertising and expensive marketing is used to create this image. However, the delivery of the brand and the customers' experience of the advertising promise are in the hands of hundreds, or even thousands, of individual employees. It is they who serve the customers and either confirm or destroy much of the image created at so much expense by the company's advertising and marketing.

In relation to proving the case that HR adds real business value, there are obvious difficulties. For example, how do you measure organisational performance over time? What indicators do you use? How do you calculate/assess the impact of specific human resource interventions? In summary, as John Storey (*Developments in the Management of Human Resources*, Blackwell, 1992) has argued, the demonstration of this causal link is fraught with immense difficulty because of the vast range of confounding variables.

Do you believe that the HR function adds real business value?

Does your boss believe it? Are line managers really swayed by the force of academic debate? The reality is likely to be somewhat different. How often have you worked with a line manager who was antagonistic to managing people well – and who did a 180-degree U-turn having 'read the literature'? Who reads the academic journals anyway?

To some extent this argument is a philosophical one. Either you believe that people are a critical organisational resource which adds real business value – or you don't (ie you essentially see people as a cost that needs to be carefully measured and controlled). It follows that in some organisations, people management as a strategic lever becomes an assumption taken for granted within management cognition.[4] Indeed, in some organisations, the idea that people are a source of competitive advantage is so integrated within mainstream management thought that the presence of a powerful and lobbying HR director and function may actually be less important. It is less important precisely because line and senior managers are capable of incorporating HR processes into their thinking in an informed way and do not require prompting or influencing by HR specialists. In reality these managers still need specialist advice in terms of implementation options, but this can be provided either by the HR function acting as an internal consultant or by external consultants who may be brought in on a flexible basis when necessary. In other organisations the fundamental belief that people add real value simply does not exist. HR managers who work in this type of organisation have to continually sell the idea that they bring relevant skills to the party.[5]

Where do you go from here?

Going forward options for the HR function

In terms of 'grabbing attention', an interesting debate is whether the HR function should take an evolutionary route ('Let's fix the today problems before we get ahead of ourselves') or focus on a 'tomorrow' agenda ('There is almost no limit to what could be done here'). While the individual elements of the nine-step model presented in this book should help you to decide this specific question, there is a general organisational principle that applies.

In order to get management attention and support for a 'new' agenda it is usually necessary to be performing above a baseline level. Where performance is significantly off par it is difficult to get support for some new initiative. In essence, performing reasonably well on the 'day job' provides a licence to experiment with more strategic initiatives. It follows that some HR teams will normally need to focus on a remedial agenda (fixing today) before the more strategic elements of the model explored in this book can be brought into play.

There is a range of possibilities in taking any HR department forward. These are summarised in Table 12.

The story so far...

Congratulations – you have now 'fixed' the resources issue and have sufficient political clout/money/people to get the job done. However, a defining point in the success of HR departments is their understanding of internal marketing – to which we now turn the spotlight.

Chartered Institute of Personnel and Development

Customer Satisfaction Survey

*We would be grateful if you could spend a few minutes answering these questions and return the postcard to CIPD. <u>Please use a black pen to answer</u>. **If you would like to receive a free CIPD pen, please include your name and address.*** IPD MEMBER Y/N

....

1. Title of book ....

2. Date of purchase: month .... year ....

3. How did you acquire this book?
☐ Bookshop   ☐ Mail order   ☐ Exhibition   ☐ Gift   ☐ Bought from Author

4. If ordered by mail, how long did it take to arrive:
☐ 1 week   ☐ 2 weeks   ☐ more than 2 weeks

5. Name of shop .... Town.. Country ....

6. Please grade the following according to their influence on your purchasing decision with 1 as least influential: (please tick)

	1	2	3	4	5
Title					
Publisher					
Author					
Price					
Subject					
Cover					

7. On a scale of 1 to 5 (with 1 as poor & 5 as excellent) please give your impressions of the book in terms of: (please tick)

	1	2	3	4	5
Cover design					
Paper/print quality					
Good value for money					
General level of service					

8. Did you find the book:
Covers the subject in sufficient depth   ☐ Yes   ☐ No
Useful for your work   ☐ Yes   ☐ No

9. Are you using this book to help:
☐ In your work ☐ Personal study   ☐ Both   ☐ Other (please state)

Please complete if you are using this as part of a course

10. Name of academic institution...

11. Name of course you are following? ....

12. Did you find this book relevant to the syllabus? ☐ Yes ☐ No ☐ Don't know

Thank you!

To receive regular information about CIPD books and resources call 020 8263 3387.

1795/05/00

Publishing Department

Chartered Institute of Personnel and Development

CIPD House

Camp Road

Wimbledon

London

SW19 4BR

Table 12
TAKING THE HR DEPARTMENT FORWARD

Options	Advantages	Disadvantages
1 Internal problem-solving approach HR Group works internally to resolve the key presenting issues within the function as they are currently perceived.	• Very quick • Visible early gains • Puts resources in most needed spots • Run with internal resources/low cost	• Limited by 'today' focus (operational rather than strategic) • Does not involve the line management team (who are often key players in the presenting issues)
2 HR re-engineering Assess effectiveness of the current key processes used and streamline them. This is a build on the problem-solving approach except that the analysis is deeper with the focus on *processes* and mapping the effectiveness of them.	• Bigger benefit to the business (short- and medium-term) • Builds additional skills into the HR team • Opportunity to learn and implement best practices – through rigorous benchmarking • Provides a base for HR department ISO 9000 accreditation (if you want to go this route)[6]	• Time-consuming • Needs external resources input • Higher cost • Harder to sell internally
3 Customer prioritisation Work on the key presenting issues detailed by the customer group (ie what the customers expect but do not currently receive from the HR function). These become key priority fixes.	• High acceptance from customers • Fairly quick • Can be completed with internal resources • Focused on value-added activities as measured from the customer perspective • Clearly highlights benefit of HR function to the business	• Tends to over-emphasise today (customers may not know what their future requirements are) • Is overly focused on a 'remedial' rather than a 'developmental' agenda • Does the appetite to go after this agenda exist? • May need external resources input/cost
4 Conduct full HR audit External/professional input into current practices. This will hold a mirror up to the current organisation.	• Brings objectivity to the audit process • Provides indirect benchmarking against other sites/excellent companies. In times of rationalisation, some HR groups find this a useful way to copperfasten the rationale for the function • Data/benchmarking comparison available to local management and to the corporation	• Excludes the line management group (possibly) • Needs external resources input/cost
5 Develop HR mission and detailed workplan Define HR function mission and world-class plan to implement it.	• Helps HR group to fully understand their own role • Provides 'road-map' for all HR activities • Can be validated by the line management team	• Time-consuming • Cost of consulting support in facilitating plan construction
6 Metrics for the function Agree a specific scorecard for the HR function.	• Allows HR to measure current performance • Builds additional skills into the HR team • Fits well with several of the earlier options	• Can promote scepticism if today is seen to be 'broken' by the internal customers – ie it can be seen as working on a low-priority issue • Can highlight under-performance very visibly

References

1   Some HR managers simply 'facilitate' the diagnosis' being done by an external consultant. This may be on the basis that consultants may have better diagnostic tools/skills. It may also make more sense politically ('You can't be a prophet in your own land'). Consultants are also more expendable if for some reason the project goes off the rails. In the words of the Turkish proverb, 'The man who tells the truth should have one foot in the stirrup.'

2   Jeffrey Pfeffer, *The Human Equation*. Boston Mass, HBS Press, 1998.

3   See for example, M. A. Huselid, 'The impact of human resource management practices on turnover, productivity and corporate financial performance', *Academy of Management Journal*, Vol. 38, No. 3: pages 635–672, 1995.

4   Lynda Gratton, Veronica Hope-Hailey, Philip Stiles and Catherine Truss, *Strategic Human Resource Management*. Oxford, Oxford University Press, 1999.

5   Which can get 'old' pretty quickly. My own (anecdotal) research on this indicates that culture misfits are a key cause of HR personnel turnover.

6   While a number of recruitment consultancies have achieved this, to my knowledge Nortel is the only company in Ireland to achieve ISO 9000 for the HR function.

7 INTERNAL MARKETING

He who whispers down a well
About the goods he has to sell
Will never make as many dollars
As he who climbs a tree and hollers.
Lord Leverhume

When HR managers bemoan the fact that the line managers 'do not support the function', the issue is often poor internal marketing – ie the theorem that 'excellence in human resource management leads to business success' has not been well established. In some cases it may be that the 'customer' (the organisation) does not want your product (well-thought-through human response strategy copperfastened by active line management support) – you may be attempting to sell a '100-per-cent beef' HR solution to a vegetarian employer! If you work for such an organisation, the sheer effort of trying to justify your existence on an ongoing basis may force you to reconsider whether you are plying your trade in the right place. In other cases the organisation may be open-minded about the relative contribution of the HR function – *but* the HR manager does not have the personal credibility to 'close the sale', or historically the case has not been made.

A key stumbling-block for many HR functions is the invisibility of the services typically provided. As a result, HR managers often lack the clout and budgets of their marketing and Information Technology colleagues. They struggle to provide concrete evidence that the policies and practices they recommend achieve tangible results and measurably contribute to organisation performance. Excellent internal marketing is a key tool to help overcome scepticism in this area.

I believe that internal marketing is a key skill – as important as some of the core functional skills we have reviewed earlier. A senior personnel manager once suggested to me that 'the best assurance for success in this business it to find yourself a good external printer. Put all of your stuff in full-colour spreads.' While cynical, it contains enough common sense to make it worth paying attention to.

Let me state a bias at the outset. No amount of packaging will overcome the non-delivery of the core HR role. Line managers will always see through gimmickry, no matter how cleverly packaged, which does not address the business fundamentals. Nonetheless, packaging and selling your product internally is a vital aspect of the HR role.

There is no sense of fairness in this debate. The image you have is the one you deserve, and it is your responsibility to manage it. In the words of Tom Davis, 'How that image may have been created, inherited or distorted by your predecessors is entirely irrelevant.'[1] Human resources managers who do not understand this were once colourfully referred to as 'melon-carriers' – the people there to help 'set up the picnic'.[2]

The creation of an internal marketing plan begins with the adoption of a service-oriented attitude – understanding the clients' needs and wants and placing them above your own. It implies well-developed listening skills, ways of identifying needs and building a collaborative HR programme to meet them. It also implies staying positive on your contribution. (One manager in a manufacturing plant where we worked was so negative that his boss nicknamed him 'Black Cloud'.)

How is the personnel department currently viewed?

One client organisation conducted an internal audit which produced the following 'snapshot' of how the function was seen.

- ❑ removed from marketplace
- ❑ heavily administration-driven, generating too much paper
- ❑ always saying no – slow to react
- ❑ somewhere to be avoided
- ❑ keeping 'top secret' files

❑ all-powerful
❑ no clear role definition.

Telling customers what HR departments actually do

Many consumers purchase products/services and subsequently use only a small percentage of the capacity/potential
benefits. In similar vein, you may need to 'educate' your
customers on the products and services available from HR
and on how you can help them to develop a high-performance
organisation.

One way to do this is to develop a comprehensive HR plan
that identifies the business issues and the specific HR initiatives that flow from it. An example of an internal HR plan is
given in Appendix B,[3] which gives a good idea of the scope of
such a document and the areas you need to cover, although the
details will differ widely between sectors and organisations.
Another, simpler, way is to show the products/services in
graphic form (see Figure 24).

Figure 24
WHAT DO WE DO IN HR?

Finding the right lever: running HR like a 'business'

As a way of internally marketing the role, some HR functions have begun to progress along the 'HR is a separate business' route.

If the HR function is set up as a stand-alone business (so the argument runs), it can deliver unmistakable/irrefutable value to the organisation.[4] Whether this is a good idea is very dependent on local circumstances. In some cases, viewing HR as a separate business may well be appropriate and an excellent discipline for the HR professionals. However, some companies simply do not have a culture of paying attention to the HR function regardless of how it is labelled or the quality of the services it offers. A key question is 'Does your organisation fundamentally support what you are trying to do?' Is there a core belief that 'people are an important asset that must be invested in – that people add real business value', or is this lip-service paid to readers of the annual report? In essence, are you working for an organisation that has a *soul*?

How can you demonstrate that you pursue best practice?

Dr Eddie Molloy is a well-respected organisational development consultant. He has considerable experience working in the area of developing HR strategy. On one assignment, the client company posed the following question: 'How would we recognise best practice in HRM?' Eddie's response is detailed in Figure 25. It provides a useful working example of the elements that constitute best practice, from the perspective of the different stakeholders.

The Molloy model is useful on two levels.

1   It gives a sight of the 'prize' to line managers who may not otherwise see the benefit of having a first-class HR system. Part of the dilemma around building this is that the 'prize' is often somewhat abstract. It may not be clear to the senior team what first-class human resource management looks like, or what benefits may flow to the organisation from developing it.

2   It copperfastens the point that excellent HR is not simply the outcome of the work of the HR department but is a

Figure 25

THE MOLLOY MODEL OF DEMONSTRATED BEST PRACTICE

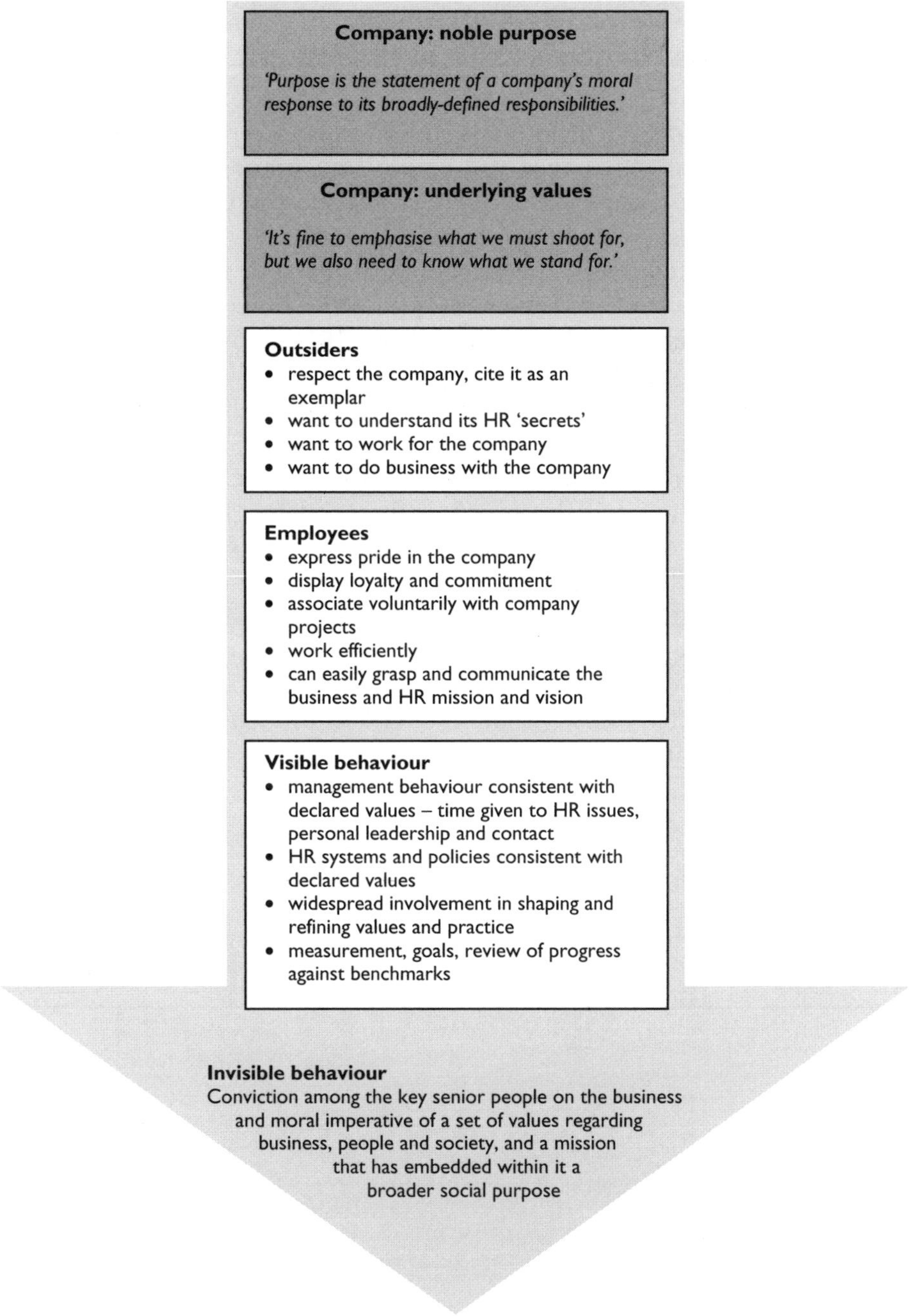

Company: noble purpose

'Purpose is the statement of a company's moral response to its broadly-defined responsibilities.'

Company: underlying values

'It's fine to emphasise what we must shoot for, but we also need to know what we stand for.'

Outsiders
- respect the company, cite it as an exemplar
- want to understand its HR 'secrets'
- want to work for the company
- want to do business with the company

Employees
- express pride in the company
- display loyalty and commitment
- associate voluntarily with company projects
- work efficiently
- can easily grasp and communicate the business and HR mission and vision

Visible behaviour
- management behaviour consistent with declared values – time given to HR issues, personal leadership and contact
- HR systems and policies consistent with declared values
- widespread involvement in shaping and refining values and practice
- measurement, goals, review of progress against benchmarks

Invisible behaviour
Conviction among the key senior people on the business and moral imperative of a set of values regarding business, people and society, and a mission that has embedded within it a broader social purpose

combined outcome of the *philosophy* and actions of the line management team *and* the quality of the HR function/team.

A shared HR vision across the management team: a key goal

Developing a turbo-charged HR system requires functional excellence allied to a pro-active line management team, and that both groups are actively committed to the development of world-class people practices. Regardless of individual brilliance, the effectiveness of the HR team is acutely determined by the context in which they work. The construction of this 'future vision' (what a first-class HR system will incorporate) has to be built up internally by the people who are responsible for it. An attempt to capture this point diagrammatically is shown in Figure 26.

The practical on-the-ground experience of people in the organisation will be much influenced by the philosophy and practices of the line management team. Excellent people strategies or HR processes will not compensate for a line management team who are not fundamentally committed to this area. In real terms the chief executive and line management team 'set the height of the bar' and the constraints within which the HR team operate. It follows that the HRM model/practices must be custom-fit to the particular organisation, based on both the

Figure 26
THE IMPORTANCE OF LINE AND HR MANAGEMENT CONGRUENCE

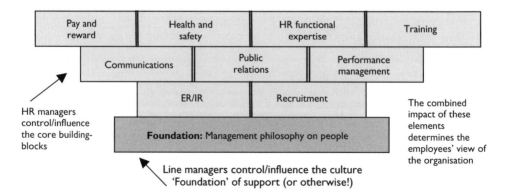

operating environment (as covered in detail earlier) *and* the underlying management philosophy.[5] While the issue of cultural fit is an important consideration for all managers thinking of moving to a new organisation, it is critically important for HR managers because it is fundamental to their personal success.

Line management roles and behaviours are critical.

Bottom line: the HR department represents a complement to the line management team – not a substitute for it.

How clear is your 'aim-point'?

Internal marketing works best when there is a defined endpoint to work towards. Vague generalities about people's being important – 'strategic assets' or 'sources of competitive advantage' – simply do not cut ice! To assist one organisation (An Gárda Síochana, the Irish police force) with this specific question we helped them develop an HR 'aim-point' – a snapshot of what the organisation might look like at a future moment in time.[6]

Building a first-class people management system: our vision

By 2003 our goal is to build a first-class policing organisation in which our members can contribute at their highest potential. We will achieve this by:

1 Recruitment
We will hire the best available talent – people with a will to succeed and the ability to work within any level in the Force. Our newest recruit is the raw material for our future success.

2 Training and education
We will offer the best training and further education opportunities of any EU police force. Members are our core resource and we will continually invest in our people, providing opportunities to learn from best practices in Ireland and from the best policing organisations in the world.

3 Performance management and personal development
We want to build an environment in which people have clear performance goals/measures and the opportunity to get feedback

on how they are doing. We want to build a work ethic following which each member individually strives to provide the best possible service to the public. We will provide an environment of equality of opportunity to all members and support their efforts to develop their career.

4 Communications and involvement

We will communicate the key targets in our Annual Policing Plan and involve all ranks in the construction of local targets. We want to build formal and informal mechanisms to continually tap into the creativity and thinking that exists throughout the organisation. The senior officers do not have a monopoly on good ideas.

5 Rewards and recognition

We will maintain our 'fair pay' stance, ensuring that the living standards of our members are maintained. We also want to develop internal systems whereby members who perform excellently can move into increasingly responsible positions. We live in a meritocracy where sustained effort and results get rewarded.

6 Employee relations

We will endeavour to provide a work climate which is built on a culture of fairness and respect for the individual. We will try to work proactively with the representative associations to ensure that issues raised get dealt with speedily. Working in partnership, our goal is to continually improve operational standards across the Force.

7 Discipline and ethics

We will continue to be a disciplined body of people working to the highest possible ethical standards. As guardians of the law we will role-model high standards in everything we do.

8 Teamwork

We wish to nurture teamwork within and across all units. Our goal is to harness the collective strengths of our 12,000+ members – all marching forward in unison – sharing positive information and learning from our mistakes.

How will we measure our success?

We will have achieved our goal when all senior ranks behave consistently with our stated philosophy, when members express pride in and loyalty to the organisation, and when external organisations come to Ireland to benchmark our human resource management practices.

Using external accreditation to support the function

Some HR departments use external accreditation to help support the function. For example, First Active (an Irish Bank) have consistently achieved the 'Excellence through People' Award from FÁS (the Irish Training and Employment Authority), and this is used internally to 'position' the function as leading-edge. While the *primary* driver in seeking this award is nominally to have an independent review, the internal marketing dimension is also important to many HR departments. The 'Excellence through People' Award system in the UK mirrors the Irish system, and is often pursued for similar reasons.

The story so far...

Being 'excellent' is not enough. You need to be able to demonstrate it to the line management team – internally marketing the function and the benefits of managing people really well. In some companies, often those with an engineering bias, you also need to be able to show continuous improvement. It is this area of measurement to which we now shift the spotlight.

References

1   'How personnel can lose its Cinderella image', *Personnel Management*, December 1987, pages 34-36.

2   I am grateful to Pat Cunneen of Analog Devices for this amusing description; in discussion with author, April 2000.

3   There is a tension here between developing a separate HR plan and seeing HR initiatives as an extension of normal business initiatives (eg the link with the business being more explicit). One way to do this is to write HR plans

with this linkage made overt/visible – working examples of this were highlighted earlier in Chapter 2. There is no correct answer on this question. It has to be addressed on a case-by-case basis.

4   See for example David Van Adelsberg and Edward A. Trolley, *Running Training Like a Business*, Forum Corporation, USA, 1999.

5   For an excellent discussion on this see Lynda Gratton, Veronica Hope Hailey, Philip Stiles and Catherine Truss, *Strategic Human Resource Management*. Oxford, Oxford University Press, 1999, pages 41–58.

6   This projection technique is individual psychology as applied to organisations. Many methods exist to do this – all with the goal of helping the organisation to 'see' the future.

8   HR METRICS

You don't have to do this – survival isn't compulsory.
W. Edwards Demming

Should we measure what we do?

In relation to measurement the HR community are often their
own worst enemies. While almost every other facet of business
life is measurable, historically there has been a reluctance to go
down this route in HR circles. The absence of measurements
leaves the function open to the jibe that 'How can you know if
it's working if you don't measure the outcome?' HR managers
struggle to justify the resources that they seek if they fail to
provide the objective measurement that both companies and
investors increasingly demand. The absence of quantification
forces HR departments to remain on the periphery of strategic
decision-making, rather than occupying the central role which
the importance of the function requires. Is this where you want
to be?

Most organisations track investment returns on physical
and financial assets – but are often ill-disciplined when they
invest in human capital. For example, how effective is your
organisation's training? Is it linked to measurable changes in
performance? Possibly your organisation is an exception, but
many companies spend up to 6 per cent of payroll on something that is not tracked to performance. Training is often
haphazard, disconnected from the organisational strategy,
delivered by many suppliers, and can be a substantial waste of
money if not properly controlled. In his book *Intellectual
Capital*, Tom Stewart quotes John Seely Brown, director of
Xerox's Palo Alto research centre:

Most companies can't tell you how much they spend on training. It took us six months to decipher – $30 million dollars a year. And one penny out of every hundred hit the mark.

Below the waterline the 'non-embracing' of a measurement system often distances the HR function from managers who have more of a quantification bias. At this point in time, I cannot think of a single, solid argument for not having measures that withstands scrutiny.[1] One chief executive of a client company captured the issue as follows:

HR the poor relation

HR is still something of a poor relation when it comes to allocating senior management time. It is interesting to compare the care and attention that goes into our evaluation of investments in business development versus our investment in management development. (See Table 13)

Table 13
INVESTMENT CONTRAST:
BUSINESS v MANAGEMENT DEVELOPMENT

Investment in business development	Investment in management development
1 High priority – close board and senior management involvement.	1 Relatively little board and senior management time commitment – at least historically.
2 One- to five-year budget and planning process.	2 One-year (often remedial) training plans.
3 Endgame is clearly specified.	3 Endgame is vague.
4 New investment thoroughly integrated with old.	4 New additions without rigorous tests for consistency.
5 Project management disciplines applied – milestones, reviews, audits, etc.	5 Absence of any rigorous project management disciplines.
6 Rigorous ROI disciplines applied.	6 Little validation of return on investment.

What areas within the HR function can be measured?

While it is difficult to measure the performance of each HR service element with unerring accuracy, measurements can be found for most aspects of the work. Once agreement is reached on what elements should be tracked and the specific metrics to be applied, it is a relatively simple process to measure performance against them. In order to increase their effectiveness in this area, some companies use external consultants, a methodology that also supports objectivity.[2]

Measurement criteria: how should we decide what to include?

At the macro level the goal is to ascertain whether the organisation is building or destroying its human capital. How well an organisation uses its intellectual, social and emotional capital is the key end goal.[3] In selecting the areas for measurement there are four major criteria:

1 *The relevance of the measure to overall business performance* – Before you begin you should ask what use the data will eventually be put to. There is little point in expending a lot of effort in data collection if the result is of little interest to the business managers.

2 *The amount of control the HR function can exercise over the particular measure* – It is generally useful to differentiate between two measures under this heading:
   a people management issues within the control of the HR function – eg length of the hiring process
   b people management issues within the control of the line management team – eg the organisational climate in particular departments.

3 *The ease of data collection* – You need to develop a mechanism to capture this data – without making this an industry in itself.[4]

4 *Data quality* – Assessing the quality of the data is the final factor to be considered under this heading. Are the numbers accurate? How good is the data integrity?

Criteria 1 and 3 alone provide a matrix of data-collection variability, as summarised in Figure 27.

Figure 27

HR DATA-COLLECTION VARIABLES

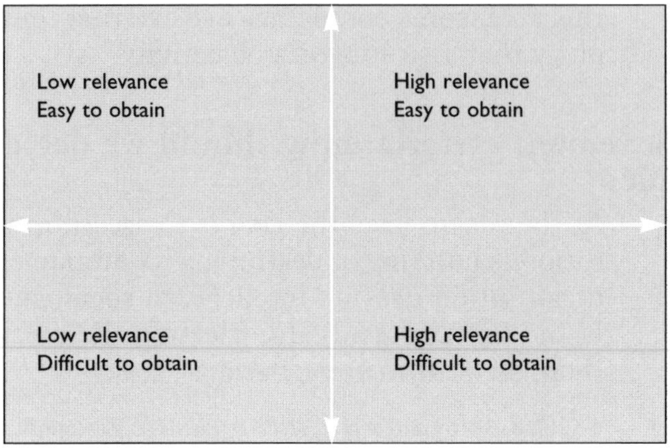

Low relevance
Easy to obtain

High relevance
Easy to obtain

Low relevance
Difficult to obtain

High relevance
Difficult to obtain

Refining the scorecard

As with most business areas, the initial attempts to construct an HR scorecard may be less than optimal. Some of the data you chose to collect may, in practice, prove to be less than useful; other data may simply be too difficult to gather. The art here is not in brainstorming the 2,000 areas in which you *could* collect data; it is in selecting the key areas that really will make a difference. In organisational terms, being excellent is not enough – you need to be excellent in areas of strategic importance, and your HR scorecard should reflect this.

Pulling it all together: making your scorecard visible

The health-care organisation SmithKline Beecham uses the term 'Our Vital Signs' to denote their business scorecard. The 'vital signs' idea is clever in that it uses language from the health-care industry which people can relate to. Other examples are car manufacturing companies which use 'dashboard' formats, or airline companies which use 'cockpits' formats. You need to decide what the 'vital signs' are for your human resource function and how best to present this information. One simple example of this process is presented in Figure 28.

Figure 28

PACKAGING THE PERFORMANCE OF THE HR FUNCTION

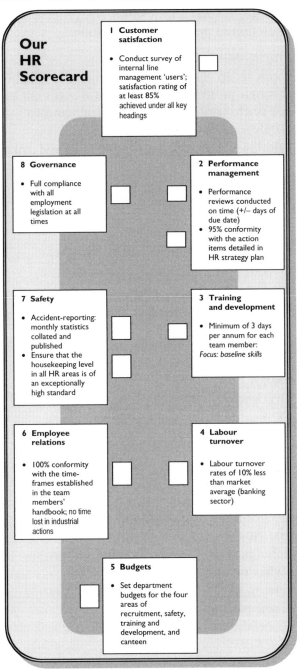

Do you want to develop an HR measurement system?

Although HR data measurements must be customised to each organisation, you can kickstart the process. Measurable items, measurements and methods include:

1 *Employee relations*

❑ Interest in employees' problems will be demonstrated through promptness of remedial action. There is to be 100-per-cent conformance to time-frames set out in the employee handbook.

❑ Employee surveys will be conducted quarterly and will achieve a feedback rating of 85 per cent+ averaged on key headings.

❑ The number of 'corrective action programmes' in progress.

2 *Climate survey*

❑ $\dfrac{\text{Overall opinion survey rating this year}}{\text{Overall opinion survey rating last year}} \times 100$

❑ The number of employee improvement suggestions (submitted/trend).

3 *Productivity index*

❑ £ sales per employee.

❑ Versus previous year.

❑ Overtime/hours worked as a percentage of normal hours/trend.

4 *Performance management*

❑ Performance reviews should be conducted on time (plus or minus five days of due date).

❑ Metrics will be developed for those working in all areas (eg reception, answering the telephone within n seconds of the first ring).

❑ Individual performance index (n people achieve a 'B' or higher rating).

❑ Performance ratings distribution (by manager or area) to assess easy/tough markers.

5 *Training investment*
- ❏ Average training costs per employee.
- ❏ Total percentage training costs – current versus previous year.
- ❏ Training of new employees at less than £5,000.00.

6 *Training and development*
- ❏ Training and development annual plan for each individual employee.
- ❏ Each team member to receive a minimum of five days' training per annum (proposed/costed versus actual).
- ❏ Movement index – the number of people doing the same job for *n* years.
- ❏ European computer 'driving licence' for *n* employees (see www.ecdl.ie for more information).

7 *Labour turnover and absenteeism*[5]
- ❏ Labour turnover is to be less than 10 per cent.

$$\left(\frac{\text{Number of employees resigned this year}}{\text{Average headcount this year}} \times 100 \right)$$

- ❏ Absence is to be less than 2 per cent.

$$\left(\frac{\text{Number of days lost through unofficial absence/sickness}}{\text{Number of days worked}} \times 100 \right)$$

- ❏ Length of service analysis (eg staff turnover in relation to length of service; staff turnover in relation to area).

8 *Safety*
- ❏ The housekeeping level in all HR areas is to be of an exceptionally high standard – our scores are to remain in the upper quartile of the monthly audit results.
- ❏ Monthly statistics are to be maintained with regard to accident reporting.
- ❏ A computerised HR database on accidents and near misses will be introduced.
- ❏ Lost-time accidents are to be reduced by 10 per cent.
- ❏ Calculation of the cost of accidents (in insurance claims, lost time, etc).

9 *Recruitment*

- Number of 'waiting days' per hire versus agreed service contract (job-fill cycle time).
- Hiring costs for individual is to be less than £5,000.00. (Details often kept of total recruitment costs – agency and own advertising – per new recruit.)
- $\dfrac{\text{Number of employees, current year}}{\text{Number of employees, previous year}} \times 100$
- Recruits selected divided by recruits interviewed.

10 *Total compensation*

- Current compensation/benefits positioning in the marketplace – 75th percentile.
- Vis-à-vis selected benchmark competitors.
- Versus previous year.
- Pay band deviations (number of employees on special deals).

11 *Employee benefits*

- Cafeteria costs divided by number of employees.
- Medical costs divided by number of employees.
- Health insurance costs divided by number of employees.
- Benefits costs as a percentage of total compensation.

12 *Headcount/staff mix/diversity*

- Headcount levels kept below n.
- Gender balance/diversity.
- Ratio of managers to front-line staff (as a percentage).

13 *Staff numbers and operating costs of the HR function*

- Salary (+ bonus) costs of those working within HR as a percentage of the organisation's total salary (+ bonus) costs.
- The ratio of HR staff to full-time employees.

14 *Succession capability/movement*

- Depth of managerial talent – eg number of Green Code candidates.
- Percentage of internal promotions versus external hires.
- Absolute number of promotions last year.

15 *Customer satisfaction*

☐ Survey of internal users of the HR function: a satisfaction rating of 85+ per cent should be achieved under all key headings.

☐ Perception of added value judged by end users (on general HR services).

☐ Customer accessibility, rated in contacts over specific duration.

☐ Response times to queries, rated as within *n* hours.

☐ The number of service level agreements (SLAs) in place with all customers.

16 *Knowledge creation/management*

☐ We have increased our depth of understanding on 'technology X' by *n* per cent.

☐ We have developed a method to cross-fertilise our thinking on 'Y'.

☐ Depth of HR staff expertise (in numbers of staff per competency).

17 *Facilities costs (per year/per specified duration)*

☐ Staff restaurant costs of £*n* (or £*n* per head).

☐ Security costs of £*n*.

☐ Building maintenance costs of £*n*.

18 *Project management specific measures*

In addition to the 'generic' measures listed above you may well have a range of individual measures for specific projects.

The story so far...

Measuring the score is a vital element in turbo-charging your HR function. Combined with the earlier steps, it allows you to move the function up a gear. Only one question remains: 'Do you have what it takes to be successful in this game?'

References

1   Other than cases in which you are aware that the performance of the HR department is terrible and you wish to hide that fact – hardly a legitimate argument.

2   For example, Nortel (Northern Telecom) use an external consultancy to administer/collate an HR service questionnaire annually, and feel this is best done by a neutral party.

3   This is a build on the ideas first put forward by Lynda Gratton, Associate Professor of Organisation Behaviour, London Business School; see *Personnel Management*, 16 December 1999.

4   At one point in my life I was responsible for collating all the lateness and absence data for a manufacturing plant with 500+ employees. This was a monthly chore which took about two full days to complete. As an experiment I subversively stopped doing it for two months, and no one noticed – which led us to revisit the entire data collation rationale and come up with a much simpler process.

5   The issue of staff retention is a complex sub-area with a number of specific measurements. For a more detailed discussion on this see Paul Mooney, *Keeping Your Best Staff: The human resources challenge in a competitive environment*, Dublin, Oak Tree Press, 1999.

9 PERSONAL IMPACT

As HR professionals the future of our organisations depends on us. We can transform that future but we must go and do it ... Don't wait for your ship to come in – row out to meet it!
Wally Russell, HR Director of Nortel

So what is the unique contribution of the HR manager?

If the role of the HR manager is simply to 'understand the business' and to develop an HR plan which dovetails with it, could the role be carried out by any business manager who is normally bright and understands the organisation? I don't believe that it can. The unique contribution of the HR manager is twofold, having both a 'skills' and a 'philosophy' component.

Skills component

The skills component is to have the knowledge/skills to enable the department to be managed in a way that takes account of the significant body of research around best organisation and people practices. Based on the earlier chapters in this book, it should be clear that this is a huge body of research and knowledge which needs full professional mastery.

Philosophy component

The philosophy component is to ensure that the needs of people in the business are brought to the table when decision-making is under way.

In essence, the HR manager is the conduit by which expertise in respect of people and of organisational behaviour is brought into the business. The HR director should also ensure that the 'conscience' of the organisation is brought to bear on particular decisions. At the Institute of Personnel and Development Exhibition in the UK (1999), Jim Mowatt, national secretary of the Transport and General Workers' Union stated it thus: 'If redundancies are necessary, people should be piped ashore with dignity – not forced to walk the plank.'

Taking stock: assessing your own development needs

The skills needed by a well-rounded HR manager have markedly changed over the past 10 years. Many senior HR professionals served their apprenticeship during a turbulent industrial relations period in the 1970s and 1980s. The needs of the function have moved on since that time, and many HR managers are almost like the Popeye cartoon – with an 'overdeveloped IR muscle' – and less development in the other elements of the function. In the words of Paul Vickery, HR manager in IBM (Dublin):

> Many personnel managers were good during the war but are not so good in peacetime.

It follows that there is usually a need to take stock of individual skill levels and the overall corporate skills base. The key questions to be addressed are outlined below and in Figure 29. The checklist of human resources competencies set out in Appendix C may also provide useful pointers.

What do I want to be when I grow up?

Strategy level

- ❑ How much time do I spend on strategy issues for the business?
- ❑ Has HR a focus/'noble vision' for the twenty-first century?
- ❑ How well is the function integrated into the rest of the business?
- ❑ How much time do I spend externally trawling for new ideas?

Figure 29

TAKING STOCK, FOR NOW AND FOR LATER

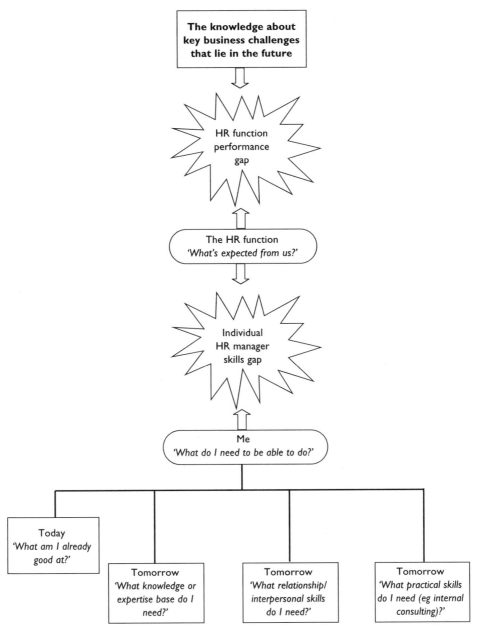

Operational level

- ❏ Do we provide a role-model for other functions?
- ❏ Do we continually ask 'Can we do this faster/cheaper?'
- ❏ Are we learning from what we did in the past?
- ❏ Are we 'customer-obsessed'?
- ❏ Does everything we do add real value?
- ❏ Do we have the resources to 'get it done'?

Personal level

- ❏ What two or three projects will I do this year?
- ❏ What am I state-of-the-art in/passionate about?
- ❏ What is my highest ambition for this operation?
- ❏ Have I 'stamped real expertise' on this (or is everyone's opinion on HR legitimate)?
- ❏ What new skills will I personally acquire this year?

It has been an enjoyable journey

Writing this book has allowed me to think about and encapsulate some of the best-practice HR efforts that we've been directly involved in or have witnessed over the past 10 years. It's tremendous to work with HR directors who 'set the bar height' at a stretch, and push to clear it. It's been an enjoyable journey, and I hope that the book has added value to your understanding of the HR function and how to 'turbo-charge' it. If it has given you a couple of new thoughts, or shattered some of the negative myths and perceptions surrounding the function, it's been worth the effort. Good hunting!

APPENDIX A
HR AUDIT TOOL

This audit comprises several operations all together making up a complete review of the HR function and its processes. These operations are:

- ❏ an organisational overview
- ❏ a review of organisational effectiveness
- ❏ a review of manpower systems
- ❏ a review of the performance appraisal system
- ❏ a review of the rewards and job size/evaluation systems
- ❏ monitoring training and development (following checklist provided).

Organisational overview

Date completed _____

Reviewer _____

Company _____

Location _____

_____

Employee composition

	Actual number	%
Exempt		
Non-exempt		
Staff		
Hourly		

Are contract/temporary staff used to supplement directs (% headcount)?

_____

Union composition

Levels/grades	_____
Number of unions	_____
Penetration percentage	_____
Contract duration/expiry date	_____

Note: Attach formal organisation chart

Sex ratios

	%		%
Male	_____	*Female*	_____
Age profile	_____	Age profile	_____
Under 25	_____	Under 25	_____
26–40	_____	26–40	_____
40+	_____	40+	_____

	%
Ratio of HR staff/total manpower	_____
Structure of HR function	_____
Supervisory span of control	_____

Organisational effectiveness review

Goal clarity
1 Describe the key goals for the organisation over the next 12 months (top managers).
2 Describe your job responsibilities in order of importance.
3 Is your role clearly defined (job description) and targeted (MBO)?
4 What are the impediments (if any) to your personal goals' being achieved?
5 What are the impediments (if any) to the organisational goals' being achieved?

Organisational structure/functioning
6 Does the current structure help in the achievement of the organisation's goals (span of control, etc)?
7 What conflicts (interpersonal/intergroup) occur frequently? Is this a 'design fault' in the organisation structure?
8 Which functions are perceived as having the most clout/power? Why is this the case? Does this negatively impact the organisational mission?

9 If you had to design a new organisation from the ground upward, how would it differ from what currently exists?
10 How would you describe the organisation's ability to change/accept new initiatives?
11 Are decisions made quickly? If not, has this posed a problem in the past?

Management style
12 What types of management meeting are held? (Frequency/duration/topics, etc.)
13 How could these be improved?
14 How well does the top team operate as a unit? Are there any general problem areas for the managerial team in the way they currently operate?
15 How would you describe the management style (autocratic $0 \longrightarrow 10$ totally participative)?
16 How would you describe your working relationship with each of the key function managers?
17 How are conflicts/differences of opinion resolved within the management group?

Social engineering
18 How would you describe the company's people management style?
19 How much time do function managers spend on the shop floor?
20 Do managers participate in company social activities? To what extent?
21 Are all managers on first-name terms with employees?
22 Is there an 'open-door' policy? If so, is it used?
23 Are there any specific human resource management issues that are preventing or hindering the company from meeting its business objectives (manpower/labour demarcations, etc)?

Manpower systems review

General
1 Is manpower forecasting formally completed (numbers, grades, requirement dates, estimated costs, etc)?
2 Is this integrated with strategic business planning (taking account of technological changes, demographic changes, legislation, etc)?
3 Is an allowance made for a percentage labour turnover, retirement, promotions, etc?

4   How/when/by whom is this updated?
5   Are job descriptions available for all internal positions? How/when/by whom are these revised?
6   Are person specifications available for all internal positions?
7   On a new recruitment assignment, how are these used (rolled-out versus re-evaluated)?
8   Are job requisition forms used for all new positions?

Candidate search
9   Does a written company policy/statement/document exist detailing the company's recruitment system?
10   How is in-house talent identified?
11   Are other company locations contacted when positions become available?
12   Are all positions posted internally? (Perceived effects?)
13   Is the company free to choose the most suitable person for the job, or do any restrictions apply (eg service, unions, etc)?
14   What is the ratio of internal to external hires (%)?
15   How are unsuccessful internal candidates counselled?
16   What is used – search consultants, direct hiring, or a combination?
17   What is the relative effectiveness of each in getting excellent candidates?
18   Are national newspapers/magazines used? What has the response rate been to date?
19   Does the recruitment source differ between grades?
20   What is the cost:benefit ratio of using consultants versus advertising/direct hiring?
21   What contacts are kept with the universities?
22   Are 'milk runs' conducted annually?
23   Are recruitment tools (videos/brochures, etc) available to attract the best talent?
24   Are relatives of current employees employed? (If restrictions apply, state degree.)
25   Of the latest 25 vacancies filled, how many went to relatives of existing employees? (Review cultural context.)
26   Is a system of management trainees in place?
27   What opportunity exists for internal candidates to participate?

Selection methodology
28   What is the normal lead-time for recruitment?
29   How are interviews set up/arranged?
30   How many interview/call-backs usually occur?

31 Who is involved in interviewing (line-personnel split, operational level of decision-maker)?
32 What formal training have these had in interviewing techniques? Is a standard interviewing format (eg patterned interviewing) used?
33 Are any selection tests used?
    a) skill-based (eg typing).   Yes/No
    b) psychological tests (type)   Yes/No
    c) assessment centres   Yes/No
34 At what stage of the selection process are the tests used? Is this the most economic point?
35 Are standard letters available for the recruitment process? (Copies?)
36 Are contracts of employment issued to all candidates?
37 Do these comply with specific employment legislation requirements (unfair dismissals, etc)?

Interview follow-up
38 Are reference checks conducted?
39 If so, by whom (format)?
40 Do all candidates undergo a medical examination prior to hiring (comprehensiveness)?

Induction/probation monitoring
41 Briefly describe the induction process if any, involved in the assimilation of new employees into the company.
42 Are new employees monitored during a probationary period? (Review contract language/formal monitoring system.)
43 Are selection test results validated by on-the-job performance?
44 Are handbooks of employment available and issued to all employees? Are these up to date? When were they last reviewed?

Labour turnover
45 What percentage labour turnover occurred within the last two years?

	Current year (rolling)	Previous year
Professional/managerial	%	%
Clerical/technical	%	%
Operators/junior	%	%

46 What proportion of the above labour turnover occurred within the first three months of employment?

47 Are exit interviews conducted (format) to analyse labour turnover by department/sex/cause, etc?

48 How do labour turnover rates compare with local companies'/companies' in the same industry?

49 What is the top team perception of the manpower planning/recruitment system? (That is, are the correct type of candidates being delivered on time/cost to the business?)

50 How could the current system be improved?

51 Are any departments currently understaffed/overstaffed against budget? (For how long/what reasons?)

Succession planning

52 Do formal succession plans exist?   Yes/No

53 For what level/grade?

54 What is the mechanism for updating these/when last reviewed/by whom?

55 What percentage of the senior (general manager and direct reports) levels currently have an identified Green Code successor?

56 Does the succession plan reflect current performance appraisal system ratings?

57 Does the succession plan drive the training and development system?

58 Are Green Code targets built into the performance objectives of all managers?

Performance appraisal system review

Current system

1 Does a formal performance appraisal system exist?

2 Does it apply to all grades of employees?

3 Does the same system apply to all grades?

4 What is the purpose of the system (historical review/forward plan/career counseling)?

5 How/when was the system developed? Has it been amended in any way?

6 How often are appraisals completed?

7 At what stage are appraisals complete (anniversary/common date)?

8 Are the appraisals completed on time? (Check sample survey.)

9 Describe the appraisal process (eg pre-meetings/employee input, HRM input, etc).

10 Is there an informal/formal follow-up? (If so, how often/format/ how monitored?)
11 Are salary adjustments made at the same time as the appraisal? (If not, what is the time-lag?)
12 Does an appeals procedure exist? How often used?

Note: Check whether a formal statement or written company policy on appraisals (employee handbook, etc) exists.

Performance goals
13 Are performance goals pre-set through MBO? Are the objectives:

written?	Yes/No
weighted?	Yes/No
based on outcomes or activitiy?	Yes/No
based on short- or longer-term goals (differentiated by grade)?	_____
a 'stretch', or easily achieved?	_____

14 Are human resource management skills (subordinate effective-ness) built into each manager's/supervisor's objectives, or is focus mainly 'technical'? (Check a selection of completed appraisal forms.)
15 How well do the performance goals match the job descriptions in place?
16 Do the performance ratings made (review a vertical-slice/lateral-slice selection) match the normal distribution curve?
17 What training has been given to managers in target objective-setting and conducting of appraisals?

timing (when?)	_____
coverage (who?)	_____
methodology (documentation back-up available; get copies)	_____
valuation of training	_____
retraining planned	_____

18 How do you ensure consistency of ratings among evaluators?
19 How well does the system drive performance levels?
20 How could the system be improved?
21 How do you deal with poor performance (level of dismissal/ lateral transfers over the last two years)?
22 Conduct a small sample survey of managers/more junior

employees to test the perception of the appraisal system (equity of goals and efforts, how well does it influence performance/ motivation?).

Rewards and job size/evaluation systems review

Reward systems review

1 What grouping/list of companies is used for compensation practices comparisons?
2 What is the rationale for this grouping? (Trade/industry/ geographical region, etc?)
3 Does a formal benefits planning system exist?
4 Who completes this, and to what timing?
5 Is a centralised listing (employee handbook, etc) available showing clearly the welfare, medical and social and other benefits available to employees?
6 Are work grades differentiated by level (exempt/non-exempt/hourly)?
7 Does the same reward system apply to each grade?
8 What is the company's marketplace positioning objective (pay/benefit levels)?
9 Is this differentiated between work grades?
10 What is the company's current positioning?
11 How are marketplace movements tracked? Documented/how often/by whom? (Check the past three marketplace surveys for detail/timing/completeness.)

Job size/evaluation review

12 Is job evaluation used as a means of determining base pay rates?
13 How are changes in job content dealt with?
14 How does job grading fit with the organisational chart?
15 Are these based on the Hay or the SI evaluation system, or other?
16 Is the method of job evaluation known and understood by employees?
17 Is there a union involvement in job grading?
18 How are internal equities managed (scales/grades/levels)?
19 Does a sex bias exist in salary earnings?
20 What are the percentage spreads
    a) within grades?   _____
    b) between grades?   _____
21 How is positioning within scales arrived at?
22 Is the reward system differentiated by performance (MBO system)?

23 What is the percentage differentiation made?
24 How are wage increases decided (individual manager/one-over-one/salary committee)?
25 Are pay/performance decisions made at the same time?
26 Are salary increase guidelines issued to managers (or how is consistency maintained)?
27 Where both unionised and non-union staff are employed, how are pay/benefit relativities managed?
28 What is the impact of formal wage negotiation on the non-union group?

Overtime working
29 Does a system exist which produces accurate data on overtime hours worked?
30 Who gets the figures, and what is done with them?
31 Is there a relativity problem with non-eligible employees?
32 Have restrictive labour practices developed associated with overtime (manning, particular jobs done only on overtime, call-out, supervision, rostering, etc)?

Reward cost trends
33 What is the total cost of salary/benefits for the business?
34 What percentage of total costs does salary/benefit costs account for?
35 What is the ratio of labour costs to unit costs of production?
36 What is the cost trend over the past two years?
37 What is the management's perception of the effect of the reward system on performance?
38 What is the employees' perception of how the pay/benefits package relates to comparable employers? How is this measured?
39 What current problems exist with the pay system? How could this situation be improved?

Note: Is the pay process detailed in writing? (Obtain copies of employee handbooks, etc.)

40. What other reward possibilities have employees sought/company pursued.
41. What benefit changes have been made in the last 24 months?

Pension checklist
42 Does a pension plan exist?   Yes/No

43 If more than one plan exists, check the employee categories covered by each.
44 If there is no pension plan in operation, check to see if the company provides for life assurance cover from the outset of employment.
45 Is the plan integrated with state benefits, and if so, how does this affect the calculation of pension and its cost in achieving the legal limit (two-thirds of final salary)?
46 Are the following terms defined:
    • pensionable pay?
    • final pensionable pay?
47 How is pension calculated?
48 What service must an eligible employee have before joining the scheme?
49 Is there an age qualification?
50 What is the normal retirement age?
51 What arrangements operate in the case of death-in-service benefit?
52 Is there a spouse's pension?
53 What provision is made for dependent children?
54 Is the scheme contributory or non-contributory? If it is contributory, what is the percentage of contribution?
55 Are there any special provisions – for example,
    • to counter inflation?
    • for transferability?
    • to top up pension to counter inflation?
56 Do trustees include worker representatives?
57 Is the plan fully funded to date?

Monitoring training and development

Training needs identification
1 How are training/development needs identified? Does the identification process take account of:
   a) current operational problems?
   b) long-term plans (impact of technological change, succession plans, etc)?
2 How is the identification of training needs conducted (format for data collection/personnel involved/ line or staff function, etc)?
3 Is a formal training plan issued?
4 Are training programmes issued by individual/by category?

5 Does this take account of the manpower planning forecast? How does this dovetail with the performance appraisal (or career development) system in place?

6 When is the identification of training needs completed/ updated?

7 How is progress on the individual training plans reviewed?

Training methodology

8 Who designs training programmes (human resources, industrial engineering, line, etc)?

9 What teaching/course design methodology is used?

10 Are job descriptions used to help with the design of the training courses?

11 Are course objectives set in behavioural terms?

12 How is training evaluated (records/exams/key action points)?

13 Are standardised training programmes available for new hires (operators/supervisors, etc)?

14 What training aids/programmes/videos, etc are in place?

15 Does the company have an established management library?

16 Who has responsibility for training personnel at the plant?

17 Have they been trained as trainers (adult learning, etc)?

18 How do you select and train training instructors?

19 Are outside consultants used for training (who/how selected/cost)?

20 Are debriefings held when participants return from external training courses?

21 Is a system of mentoring in place?

22 Are cross-functional/country transfers used/encouraged?

23 Is there a managerial bias in the current training expenditure?

24 Are career development reviews/sessions held with employees?

25 Are formal career planning seminars run internally?

26 Are training needs linked with individual career aspirations?

27 Has any formal training ever been given to managers with regard to personal/subordinate career planning?

28 How many 'sub-standard' employees have had to be retrained or transferred to other jobs in the last 12 months?

Training budget

29 What is your current training budget? How is the expenditure level decided?

30 Is a training budget in place (% or £)?

31 How much (% of payroll or £) has been spent on training and development in the last 12 months?

32 How many man-days have been spent on training in the last 12 months?
33 Are overall training costs increasing or falling?
34 If increasing, are economies being achieved in other areas (higher output, increased quality, fewer personnel, etc)?
35 Does the company support educational assistance? Are there written guidelines on this?
36 What percentage of employees are currently undergoing job-related studies at an external institution?

Training evaluation
37 How effective are the training, development and career planning activities in driving performance? Explain.
38 How effective are the training, development and career planning activities in preparing people for selection and placement in new positions in the organisation? Explain.
39 What is the management perception of the training/development function in terms of effectiveness in delivering needed short- and long-term skills to the business?

APPENDIX B
HUMAN RESOURCES
STRATEGIC PLAN

This strategic plan comprises a short introductory section intended as a statement of intent – the intent being to derive a plan for transforming the organisation of the HR function within a company to become more forward-looking and yet more people-oriented – and a much longer section made up of actual strategies to achieve that end. The strategies involved are:

1 A focused recruitment and staffing plan
   (including notes on the strategic goal)
2 A strategy to drive performance management
   (including a note on the management of underperformance)
3 A strategy for selective training and development
4 A strategy to effect positive employee relations
   (including notes on devolving ownership of HR to line management, on ensuring clarity of the responsibilities of specific roles, on safety issues, on social activities and sporting events, and on effective problem-solving structures)
5 A strategy for introducing an HR information system
6 A strategy for revamping the communications system generally
   (including an annual communications planner checklist)
7 A strategy to ensure payroll and cost-control effectiveness
   (including notes on benefits and non-monetary compensation).

For the purposes of this book, the name of the company for which this plan was originally drawn up has been changed to 'Bank Company'.

Understanding the business context

Bank Company mission	Bank Company vision
To grow our residential mortgage market share to 20%, to grow our ROCE to 20% and to reduce our CIR to less than 50%, all by year end 2002, and to grow earnings/share by average 10% per annum.	Focused on building high-quality shareholder returns by being the pre-eminent home loan provider in the growing Irish market and a significant niche provider in the UK market through building on long-term customer relationships by the provision of credit, investment and insurance products which enhance our customers' wealth.

Bank Company is now competing head-to-head with the biggest and best mortgage providers in Ireland and internationally. We are moving into a faster, tougher business environment. While there is no doubt that we have the organisational capability to prosper in this arena, it will not simply 'happen'. We need to understand the new rules and personally commit to the performance levels required to ensure success.

The offer to our external customers has now been decided. The 'thinking phase' is over; we now need to deliver. Internally, the management team need to provide direction ('fog clearance') and leadership through personal role-modeling. We also need to provide the environment and the tools for every staff member to do their job effectively. We are going head-to-head with the best in a lean, tough business. Our mental *attitude* will determine where we come in the race. There is no room for passengers.

'Upping a gear': turbo-charging our performance
To achieve our ambitious targets, we need to 'up a gear' in a focused and determined way. We have set ambitious targets for ourselves (they have not been imposed externally). We have had the confidence to go public with the numbers and with our aspiration to become a world-class HR function. Now that we have made the commitment, it is a mountain which we have to climb. There is a lot at stake for all of us.

Transforming our HR organisation will not be a 'clean' process.

We will experience inevitable tensions and anxieties which accompany change on this scale. There will be disagreement and debate on the way forward. Inevitably we will make wrong calls and will have to be prepared to start over in some areas.

Through all of this we must keep an abiding belief in the fact that Bank Company is moving forward. We cannot and will not settle for second-best. This plan provides the HR 'harness' to move the entire organisation forward.

The human resources response to the business challenges

A restatement and amplification of the human resources mission:

For Bank Company:
- A demonstrated understanding of the business strategy and how our products align with it
- A talented flow of people at all organisational levels, the raw material for our future growth
- A cost-effective HR service with lower pro rata costs than any competitor organisation
- A catalyst for change and continuous development and learning throughout Bank Company.

For managers:
- Responsive and high-quality internal customer service
- A conduit for best-practice thinking in relation to managing people
- An expert support role when needed
- Strategies to help our line management partners retain their best performers.

For staff:
- The opportunity for personal development and growth – we will facilitate staff in building a successful career
- Ease of access to career development and personal counselling through a highly visible service
- We will ensure that key human resource issues are continually represented on the management agenda
- We will endeavour to provide a positive work climate built on a culture of fairness.

For ourselves (the HR team):

❏ The opportunity to work within a world-class HR function with clear performance targets and measurement

❏ A professional standard of excellence in everything we do

❏ The development of a high-performance team which leads by example in the effective management of staff.

	Strategy 1: Focused recruitment and staffing plan			
Policy statement: *Our recruitment strategy uses the notion of an 'ideal candidate' to ensure that all vacancies are filled by excellent candidates. Recruiting 'tomorrow's talent' is a key managerial task – the efforts we make in this area will reflect this. At the same time we do not want to 'overhire' people for the available jobs. 'Fit' is the key watchword.*				
Number	*Project*	*Timeframe*	*Owner*	
1.1	Develop a recruitment flowchart (with lead times, etc) which sets out the parameters within which the various steps of the process will be actioned (HR and line managers will be obliged to operate).			
1.2	Draw up a profile of the type of individuals Bank Company wants to target (eg avoid over-recruitment). Specifically, at branch level, we will pursue a two-tier recruitment strategy with supporting salary scales and incentive plans. See Table 14.			
1.3	Sourcing will include developing the strategic sources for team members at both levels. This includes formal links with secondary schools, post-leaving-certificate colleges, FAS-targeting the long-term unemployed, and application forms in branches.			
1.4	Provide an incentive to internal staff to source excellent candidates.			
1.5	Identify one or two recruitment agencies with which we will develop a strategic partnership relationship. Brief them on the recruitment methodology/candidate profiles required, etc.			
1.6	Provide training in interviewing skills for all managers involved in recruitment (this should include an overview of employment legislation). Four courses over next 12 months.			
1.7	Develop a behavioural interviewing model/psychometric testing for all hiring which meets the criteria detailed above.			
1.8	Develop/use standard pre-employment reference screening for all employees.			
1.9	Provide pre-employment medical checks for all new hires/ permanent staff.			
1.10	Develop/install a systematic probation-monitoring system and rigidly adhere to it.			

Table 14
RECRUITMENT: OUR TWIN-TRACK APPROACH

Track	Role	Position	Salary range	Career
1	Processing/ transactions	Teller	£x – £y	A
2	Sales	Loans adviser / Investment adviser	£a – £b	B

Flexible staffing: the goal

The nature of our business means that permanent staff must be supplemented by a group of temporary employees. Our efforts are geared to ensuring that people receive excellent treatment during their stay at Bank Company and leave the company with an enhanced set of skills.

Number	Project	Timeframe	Owner
1.11	Develop clear company policy on the numbers of permanent as against temporary staff at each retail location and the CSC. Use a standard manpower-planning template to assist in this.		
1.12	Develop a procedure on how to handle hiring and layoffs, and communicate this to all temporary staff as required.		
1.13	Develop a means of keeping employees informed of changes which impact on job security, and the reasons for any such changes.		
1.14	Communicate to all Bank Company managers the message that people on temporary contracts are to be treated as part of the Bank Company family.		
1.15	Continue operation of flexible working hours policy; modify as appropriate.		
1.16	**Retention plan:** Conduct fully comprehensive retention analysis, eg goal is to reduce labour turnover from x% to y%.		
1.17	Conduct exit interviews with all departing staff. Use a standard format to assess underlying reasons.		
1.18	**Equality and diversity:** Establish steering committee and ensure that equality policy is developed. The positive action programme will include awareness workshops.		
1.19	Conduct internal audits to ensure that the elements of the equality policy are working as intended – eg flexible working.		
1.20	Roll out EEA/CIPD manual and video on diversity and establish informal network.		

Strategy 2: Driving performance management

Policy statement: *Bank Company is a meritocracy where performance determines progress. A critical task for each manger is to ensure that her/his people perform at optimum level. There are no passengers on the team. The revised performance management system will apply to all staff – from the managing director to the newest hire.*

Number	Project	Timeframe	Owner
2.1	Design revised performance management system for the operation (exact formats to be followed, etc).		
2.2	Train all managers in the use of the new system (performance planning, performance monitoring and performance appraisal).		
2.3	Brief all recipients in how the system works and what is expected of them.		
2.4	Monitor managers' conformity with meeting the due dates, the quality of documentation, etc.		
2.5	Monitor participants' 'acceptance' of the performance ratings and solicit feedback on how well the overall system is working.		
2.6	Develop a method to 'fast-start' all new employees to ensure that they begin to perform in the shortest possible timeframe.		
2.7	Ensure intimate involvement with the line management team. Review organisational implications of business process improvement, new systems.		

Managing underperformance

Goal: *Team members are entitled to open and honest feedback. If performance falls below accepted standards, staff should be informed and given the opportunity to improve. Continued underperformance is not a sustainable option.*

Number	Project	Timeframe	Owner
2.8	Working with the line managers, develop an 'early warning' monitoring system which will indicate when a team member's standard of performance is falling below par, and an action planning system to address this. The HR department will be responsible for monitoring this procedure.		
2.9	Develop a listing of current underperformers and construct remedial/or outplacement action plans.		

Figure 30

HOW THE SYSTEM WILL OPERATE

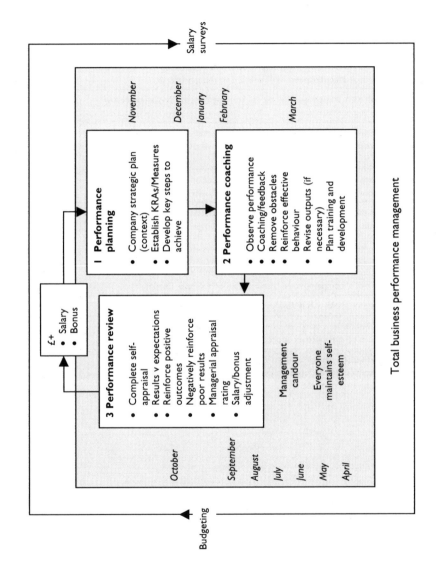

Total business performance management

Strategy 3: Selective training and development

Policy statement: *In the current year, our concentration will be to provide Bank Company team members with the knowledge and skills required for their present role – the onus on developing them for future/expanded roles within the company will be with staff themselves. Micro-skilling will enable the day job to be clinically executed.*

Number	Project	Timeframe	Owner
3.1	Develop a site-wide new employee-orientation programme (Phase 1 on first day, followed by Phase 2 one month later).		
3.2	Establish a company-wide annual training budget. Stay at or below this.		
3.3	Use systematic training modules to train staff for key positions (developed centrally by local instructors who work as part of the line management team).		
3.4	Communicate the policy on further education to all staff. Encourage people to peruse this in their own time.		
3.5	Provide a full range of training on office automation so as to continuously develop the PC literacy of employees on standard Bank Company packages.		
3.6	Complete annual analysis of training needs, which will include customer care for all employees. The result is to be the development of a company-wide training plan in a simple format.		
3.7	Conduct 'make v buy' analysis on all training activities.		
3.8	Review current usage of branch manuals/video, and update/scrap/revise as appropriate.		
3.9	Continue to input training resources 'into the line' and out of the central location. Continue dotted-line link to the centre to ensure consistency of effort.		

Strategy 4: Positive employee relations

Policy statement: *Bank Company will be characterised by an absence of employee relations conflict. We endeavour to have a direct, positive relationship with all employees and a good working relationship with SIPTU. Employee relations assistance and HR technical support will be provided to line managers in a way which does not diminish their stature or undercut their authority.*

Number	Project	Timeframe	Owner
4.1	Minimise status. Ensure that no distinctions are allowed to develop between different sections of the workforce.		
4.2	Task each senior manager with sitting among different workgroups in the restaurant and constantly communicating the company strategy.		
4.3	Ensure clear roles and responsibilities for all groups. The goal is zero ambiguity on job roles.		
4.4	Provide managers and supervisors with guidelines/training regarding the maintenance of a positive employee relations climate, how to communicate with employees regarding contract comparison, etc.		
4.5	Each manager is to be able to clearly communicate the Bank Company philosophy of managing the employment relationship directly with employees.		
4.6	Managers are to be tasked to attend funerals/mark other significant occasions in employees' lives.		
4.7	Design/run annual staff opinion surveys which help to surface problems/ER issues. Develop prospect plans to 'close out' on these.		
4.8	Establish an informal information network to ensure that particular 'irritants' continuously mentioned by team members are actioned.		

Devolve responsibility for human resources: the goal is line management ownership of HR

Number	Project	Timeframe	Owner
4.9	Each line manager should know individual employees (first-name basis, family situation, interests, aspirations, etc).		
4.10	Establish HR/line management forum. Ensure consistency throughout the line management group in the treatment of employees by biannual human resource/line managers meetings at all sites. The goal is to publish minutes of meetings for cross-company comparison. Each HR manager is to 'sponsor' five sites.		
4.11	Develop quiz for line managers on the contents of the new employee handbook.		
4.12	Ensure 'role clarity' for line managers, HR managers and employees (see below).		

Clarity of responsibilities' personnel, line management and employee roles			
Area of focus	**Line management role**	**Human resources role**	**Employee role**
1 Communications	To keep all employees informed of what is happening in the business and locally	To develop the communications 'plumbing system' To centrally prepare communications materials for use by line managers	To keep themselves informed of what is happening in the business and locally To participate fully in all communications forums To make issues of concern or interest known to the management team
2 Performance review	To set goals for all staff, to provide feedback and coaching on an ongoing basis and to comply with all due dates in the performance management system	To design a fully effective performance management system and to 'ride shotgun' on its implementation	To set stretch targets To meet/beat the targets set To continually search for better methods
3 Employee discipline	To confront employees with under-performance and to follow the corrective action procedures	To act as a 'champion' for the individual's case, including helping her/him to present a solid case to management	To strive at all times to meet objectives set To be open to feedback on performance issues To diligently tackle areas of non-performance

Safety			
The goal: *To maintain a safe and healthy working environment. Our target is to become an accident-free operation.*			
Number	**Project**	**Timeframe**	**Owner**
4.13	Using external expertise, conduct a comprehensive evaluation of the current safety levels. This will involve looking at such issues as medical facilities, accident/incident analysis reporting, hazards review, etc.		
4.14	Develop a comprehensive safety plan which includes provision for the establishment of a safety committee at the CSC.		
4.15	Publicise the safety statement company-wide.		
4.16	Train personnel in fire safety; fire wardens in place at all locations.		
4.17	Raise the consciousness level in all operations with regard to safety, health, welfare and security at work. All programmes to be developed centrally/run locally by line management team.		
4.18	Develop 'positive incentive' safety recognition programme.		

Sports and social activities			
The goal: *To maintain an active sports and social club which maximises the participation of all members/welds a common identity among staff at all levels of the organisation.*			
Number	**Project**	**Timeframe**	**Owner**
4.19	Conduct benchmark visits to the best S&S clubs in Dublin (how do they maximise participation, what were the most successful events, etc).		
4.20	Review current method of funding and annual budget v benchmarks.		
4.21	Ensure senior HR staff actively participate on the S&S committee (rotational post).		
4.22	Draw up an annual list of events.		
4.23	Ensure that senior managers are represented at each event by constructing a rota for attendance. Attendance level led by HR executives.		
4.24	Launch formal employee assistance booklet/programme.		

Effective problem-solving structures			
Policy statement: *Our goal under this heading is to resolve all issues as speedily as possible and at the lowest appropriate level within the organisation hierarchy.*			
Number	**Project**	**Timeframe**	**Owner**
4.25	Communicate the problem-solving procedure to all employees and devise a method to test that the structure is understood.		
4.26	Ensure that all members of the management team are aware of their responsibilities under this heading (include in the biannual line/HR briefings).		
4.27	Find ways to merchandise this throughout the operations (eg include it as a standard item on the noticeboards).		
4.28	Review and select one or more informal avenues for team members to vent problems or concerns (suggestion-/question-box, MBWA, open-door policy, etc).		
4.29	Successfully negotiate movement to new premises.		

Strategy 5: Introduce HR information system

Policy statement: *Our goal is to develop a first-rate information system which allows line managers instant access to the data they need to run the business. It will also provide staff with access to information which they need to help them manage their own careers.*

Number	Project	Timeframe	Owner
5.1	Introduce computerised HR database. Identify appropriate software package.		
5.2	Source a 12-month project person to install all data on the new system.		
5.3	HR information system to be signed off. Installation and inputting of key data.		
5.4	Training programme for users in HR and training and development to commence.		
5.5	Key source of information on individual performance, competencies and qualifications.		
5.6	Personnel records. Decide on a method to keep these fully up to date.		
5.7	Establish service-level agreements to cover recruitment (selection, replacement, internal movement), training days, including induction. Ensure training/IT service-level agreement in place. HR information to be provided to divisions. Staff-level agreements with divisions.		

Strategy 6: Revamp communications system			

Policy statement: *Open and direct communication is a hallmark of the way we operate. Our communications system is designed to send information through the organisation and to facilitate the movement of information upwards. This system helps to ensure that people make decisions on the basis of good information. Don't wait until you are told – if you want to know, ask!*

Number	Project	Timeframe	Owner
6.1	Construct a formal business communication plan to ensure that employees receive timely information. (See Annual communications planner, below.)		
6.2	Monitor all communications meetings to check for compliance with the company business communication plan.		
6.3	Establish a system whereby minutes of communications meetings are distributed to the HR manager and the issues which surface are addressed and posted on the noticeboards. All information must be fed back to HR by the department manager within 24 hours of the communication meeting's being held.		
6.4	Delegate responsibility for ensuring that the information included on noticeboards has a defined 'shelf-life' and is kept up to date.		
6.5	Distribute the completed employee handbook and monitor feedback from employees.		
6.6	Target specific individuals who would be helpful in steering the grapevine pro-company.		
6.7	Ensure senior management conduct face-to-face meetings with team members who work on the evening/night shifts. (A feature of the new processing/back office environment?)		
6.8	Continue to use 'people first' as an update mechanism for significant company events. The goal is 26–30 issues in the current year.		
6.9	Move communications personnel/resources to report directly to HR.		

Annual communications planner					
	What	**Purpose**	**Frequency**	**Attendees**	**Duration**
Operational agenda	1 Operations review	Operational issues/plan review/ measurement. Special projects/ deviations from plan/ interpretations/ highlights	Weekly	Executive team	1 to 2 hours
	2 Operational review with each function manager '1-on-1'	Operational issues/plan review	Monthly	MD/function managers	1 hour
	3 Strategic plan review: Executive group meeting	Trouble-shooting/cross-fertilise on strategy issues	Bimonthly	Executive team	3 hours
	4 Departmental-level strategic plan review	Communications and company performance/ accounts/special projects deviations from plan/ interpretations/ highlights	Bimonthly	Direct reports and their reports	1 to 2 hours
	5 Performance v plan. Update presentation to management group.	Review of plan/update on strategy. Open questions and answers	Quarterly	MD/function and line managers	2.5 hours
	6 Performance effectiveness programme	Clear plans/ personal development/ feedback performance review	Quarterly	Manager/ subordinate	1 to 2 hours
Strategic agenda	7 Strategic planning	Planning for tomorrow/ organisation/ effectiveness/ succession planning	Quarterly	MD and line and relevant support functions	1 day
Communications agenda	8 Communications update	General communications update/company performance/ key issues	Twice per year	All staff	2 to 3 hours
	9 Branch meetings	General communications update/company performance/key issues	Bimonthly	Branch managers/ local staff	1 hour

Strategy 7: Payroll and cost-control effectiveness			
Policy statement: *Median marketplace compensation is our target. We will ensure that salaries do not fall behind the marketplace average through proactively monitoring marketplace salary movements.*			
Number	*Project*	*Timeframe*	*Owner*
7.1	Define Bank Company's exact salary objective relative to market average and agree this with executive team.		
7.2	Develop competitive survey market (the companies with which we are in the same league).		
7.3	Conduct benchmark surveys (either directly, participate or buy-in) and publish results within executive team.		
7.4	Ensure that employees understand and accept the market positioning wage concept as a fair way to compensate.		
7.5	Deliver total compensation training (salaries plus benefits) for Bank Company's senior managers to ensure their understanding/full support.		
7.6	Develop total compensation communications materials for all staff.		
7.7	Develop a profit-sharing programme which will 'kick in' provided specific performance targets are met.		

Benefits/non-monetary compensation

The goal: *To ensure that benefits do not fall behind the marketplace average through proactively monitoring movements.*

Number	Project	Timeframe	Owner
7.8	Construct a benefits package that is regarded by employees as being as good as/better than matched employers offer.		
7.9	Cite meaningful local examples that demonstrate employee treatment that is as good as/better than standard employee contract provisions.		
7.10	Consider a range of innovative employee benefits which would be low-cost/high-return (eg fitness programmes, nutrition, stop-smoking prizes).		
7.11	Produce annual benefit statements for all Bank Company employees.		
7.12	**Staff restaurant:** In addition to providing an excellent base-line service, charge canteen management with maintaining it a 'fun' place to eat at work.		
7.13	**Cost reduction strategy:** Devise appropriate training/employee involvement mechanism to be run throughout the company. The goal is to reduce operating costs by 20%, compared to previous year.		
7.14	Closedown *n* branches without industrial disruption with a smooth transfer of the business to other branch outlets.		

APPENDIX C
HRD COMPETENCIES

This appendix focuses on the competencies that are required in an organisation and that the human resources department should be aware of, even if individuals are not confident of possessing all of them themselves.

The competencies are:

- technical
- business
- interpersonal
- intellectual.

Technical competencies

Technical competencies are functional knowledge and skills.

- adult learning understanding – knowing how adults acquire and use knowledge, skills and attitudes; understanding individual differences in learning
- career-development theories and techniques and methods used in career development; understanding their appropriate uses
- competency-identification skill – identifying the knowledge and skills requirements of jobs, tasks and roles
- computer competence understanding or using computer applications
- electronic-systems skill – having knowledge of functions, features and potential applications of electronic systems for the delivery and management of HRD (such as computer-based training, interactive video and satellite networks)
- facilities skill – planning and co-ordinating logistics in an efficient and cost-effective manner

- objectives-preparation skill – preparing clear statements that describe desired outputs
- performance-observation skill – tracking and describing behaviours and their effects
- subject-matter understanding – knowing the content of a given function or discipline being addressed
- training and development theories and techniques understanding – knowledge of the theories and methods used in training; understanding their appropriate use
- research skill – selecting, developing and using methodologies such as statistical and data collection techniques for formal inquiry.

Business competencies

Business competencies have a strong management, economics or administration base.

- business understanding – knowledge of how the functions of a business work and relate to each other, knowing the economics impact of business decisions
- cost:benefit analysis skill – assessing alternatives in terms of their financial, psychological and strategic advantages and disadvantages
- delegation skill – assigning tasks responsibility and authority to others
- industry understanding – knowing the key concepts and variables that define an industry or sector; they might include critical issues, economic vulnerabilities, measurements, distribution channels, inputs, outputs and information sources
- organisation behaviour – understanding organisations as dynamic, political, economic and social systems that have multiple goals; using that larger perspective as a framework for perceiving and influencing events and change
- organisation-development theories and techniques – knowing the techniques and methods used in organisation development; understanding their appropriate use
- organisation understanding – knowing the strategy, structure, power networks, financial position and systems of a specific organisation
- project management skill – planning, organising and monitoring work for the purposes of delivering a specific output
- records-management skill – sorting data in an easily retrievable form.

Interpersonal competencies

Interpersonal competencies have a strong communication base.

- ❑ coaching skill – helping individuals recognise and understand personal needs, values, problems, alternatives and goals
- ❑ feedback skills – communication of information, options, observations and conclusions so that they are understood and can be acted upon
- ❑ group-process skill – influencing groups so that tasks, relationships and individual needs are addressed
- ❑ negotiation skill – securing 'win-win' agreements while successfully representing a special interest in a decision
- ❑ presentation skill – presenting information orally so that an intended purpose is achieved
- ❑ questioning skill – gathering information from and stimulating insight in individuals and groups through the use of interviews, questionnaires and other probing methods
- ❑ writing skill – preparing written material that follows generally accepted rules of style and form, is appropriate for the audience, is creative, and accomplishes its intended purpose.

Intellectual competencies

Intellectual competencies are knowledge- and skills-related to thinking and processing of information.

- ❑ data-reduction skill – scanning, synthesising and drawing conclusions from data
- ❑ information-searching skill – gathering information from printed and other recorded sources; identifying and using information specialists and reference services and aids
- ❑ model-building skill – conceptualising and developing theoretical and practical frameworks that describe complex ideas in understandable, usable ways
- ❑ observation skill – recognising objectively what is happening in or across situations
- ❑ self-knowledge – knowing one's personal values, needs, interests, styles and competencies, and their effects on others
- ❑ visioning skills – projecting trends and visualising possible and probable futures and their implications.

INDEX